WHAT IS INTERNATIONAL RELATIONS?

Knud Erik Jørgensen

B BRISTOL
UNIVERSITY
PRESS

First published in Great Britain in 2022 by

Bristol University Press
University of Bristol
1–9 Old Park Hill
Bristol
BS2 8BB
UK
t: +44 (0)117 954 5940
e: bup-info@bristol.ac.uk

Details of international sales and distribution partners are available at
bristoluniversitypress.co.uk

© Bristol University Press 2022

British Library Cataloguing in Publication Data
A catalogue record for this book is available from the British Library

ISBN 978-1-5292-1096-5 hardcover
ISBN 978-1-5292-1097-2 paperback
ISBN 978-1-5292-1099-6 ePub
ISBN 978-1-5292-1098-9 ePdf

The right of Knud Erik Jørgensen to be identified as author of this work has been
asserted by him in accordance with the Copyright, Designs and Patents Act 1988.

Cover design by Blu Inc
Front cover image: jr korpa – unsplash.com

Contents

List of Figures, Tables and Box

Figures

Tables

Box

List of Abbreviations

BCCIS	British Coordinating Committee for International Studies
BISA	British International Studies Association
BSIT	Bristol Studies in International Theory
EISA	European International Studies Association
EU	European Union
HPS	History, Philosophy and Sociology
IPE	international political economy
IPR	Institute of Pacific Relations
IPSA	International Political Science Association
IPT	international political theory
IR	International Relations
ISA	International Studies Association
ISC	International Studies Conference
JAIR	Japan Association of International Relations
KAIS	Korean Association of International Studies
NISA	Nordic International Studies Association
TIP	theory of international politics
TRIP	teaching, research, and international policy
UNESCO	United Nations Educational, Scientific and Cultural Organization
WISC	World International Studies Committee

Preface

What is International Relations? is a guidebook for scholars who practise the discipline, regardless of whether they focus on research or teaching, a guidebook that takes independent travellers to conceptual locations that are often mentioned but rarely explored. It puts contemporary sights into historical context while also suggesting future directions. It is not a textbook, though I do believe advanced students will benefit from reading it.

This book began, in operational terms, with a publisher's invitation to have a meeting during the European International Studies Association's (EISA) 12th Pan-European Conference on International Relations in Prague in September 2018. As is well known in the trade, meetings with publishers can be consequential, so for 30 months *What is International Relations?* was on my to-do list. In a wider sense, I guess the process of collecting material for the book began when I joined Aarhus University to prepare a PhD thesis. Or did the process perhaps begin when I attended my first British International Studies Association (BISA) conference during stormy, rainy days in December 1989. Or perhaps when I began organizing academic workshops, the first one at the time of events in Beijing's Tiananmen Square. In this wider sense, the process of preparation includes participatory or direct observation, though without guidance from anthropological methodological procedures and most likely characterized by limited self-reflection, specifically concerning the unknown unknowns.

Preparing the manuscript has been an exciting experience not least due to the puzzle it is that we have the most contending perspectives on the discipline. On the one hand, we have those who consider the discipline mature and fully accomplished, cherishing the achievements of more than a century. On the other hand, we have those who call for the discipline to be demolished, encouraging us to forget international relations (IR) theory, or who have a principled problem with science as such, which following their conventions always should be 'science'. Notably, these contending perspectives just apply to those who consider IR a discipline. Then there are those who do not recognize the discipline, for instance suggesting it is a limitless interdisciplinary field of study. Is it really the same discipline that can be interpreted so radically differently? What is the balance between facts and normative preferences? To analyse the puzzle, which is characterized by multiple facets, I realized at some point that it would be pointless to consider the dilemma and opt for one of the alternatives. Instead, it seemed more meaningful to go for the third option, that is, to reject the dilemma. In this context, let me just admit that the choice of rejecting dilemmas is based on the assumption that choosing one of the two options is both unnecessary and increasingly unproductive.

During the process of examining the main positions of the debates and identifying ways forward, I began to see that the rationale of satisfying conventional perspectives was limited. Indeed, it would be a downright failure if I only delivered what an unspecified 'many readers' might expect. As highlighted in the conclusion, I believe with Martin Wight that one of the main purposes of university education is to escape from the Zeitgeist, not to nurture it. How misleading, and really boring, it would be to interpret the last 100 years with the help of one of the contemporary fringe compasses. In this context, I am convinced that future disciplinary historians will be harsh on some of the early 21st-century developments, for instance, the trend a colleague calls the 'obscurantist turn' in IR.

The essay in this book is intended to be what essays are supposed to be, that is, a tentative and suggestive discussion. Moreover, it is a mixture of the objective and subjective essay, the latter containing personal musings about the discipline, the former based on numerous observations on various subjects. I leave it to readers to determine the balance between the objective and subjective dimensions. Finally, I would not be surprised if one of my commentators got it right in labelling it 'a very European book'. Actually, it would confirm Karl Mannheim's idea about the *Standortgebundenheit* of scholars, that is, their embeddedness in the environment in which they live and work. The book was prepared in different European locations, ranging from a village (Alken) in Denmark, the island of Symi in Greece, and Izmir in Turkey. In addition, it draws on experiences from living and working in different countries and attending conferences in Europe, North America and Asia. COVID-19 lockdowns in Denmark and Turkey helped me focus, though I will never be thankful for their limits on freedom of movement.

I am most grateful to the five anonymous reviewers who read either the original book proposal or one of the half- or three-quarter-baked manuscripts. My language editor, JJ, has the special skill of knowing what I want to write but sometimes do not, so I was most fortunate to be able to again draw on his editing. I am particularly thankful to Morten Valbjørn, Mette Skak, Mateusz Filary-Szczepanik and Feride Asli Ergül Jorgensen, from whom I received invaluable comments on one of the last draft versions of the manuscript. They all prompted me in different ways to reconsider and improve, by means of accommodation or entrenchment. At Bristol University Press, I would like to express my appreciation to Stephen Wenham, Caroline Astley and Phylicia Ulibarri-Eglite for their patience, support and professionalism. Mathias Elkjær Christensen helped me bring order to the bibliography and Annette Bruun Andersen gave me much valuable help in preparing the typescript for the publisher. My greatest gratitude goes to Asli whose encouragement, wit, love and patience made my excursions into the genesis and progress of the discipline both viable and enjoyable.

Introduction

Little did the founders of the discipline know that they would succeed beyond their wildest imagination in creating a scientific discipline of International Relations, which has been characterized by one of its premier practitioners as 'fully-fledged, full-blown, autonomous, intellectually legitimate and accomplished' (Puchala, 2003: 273).[1] In short, their accomplishment is not a failed intellectual project or an anything-goes interdisciplinary field but a genuinely mature discipline. Little could they have known the swings and turns the discipline would take, including its defeats and victories, and the variety of trajectories that would unfold around the world.[2] Least of all could they have imagined how profoundly the world and global affairs would change, and thus how dynamic the discipline would have to be, constantly reinventing itself to face new challenges or old challenges in new circumstances. While the founders of the discipline can be excused for not knowing what the future would bring, contemporary scholars have less excuse for not knowing or understanding the different varieties of the discipline across time, space and linguistic boundaries. The rationale of this book is, thus, to examine the past in order to set directions for the future and to function as a guide for those practising the discipline, rendering it possible to avoid the experience of Monsieur Jourdain in Molière's play *Le bourgeois gentilhomme*, 'Par ma foi! il y a plus de quarante ans que je dis de la prose sans que j'en susse rien' ('What!? I've been speaking prose for over 40 years without knowing it!'). In other words, for those who practise the discipline without knowing it, welcome to the discipline.

The timing for such an enterprise – interpretation, guidance and setting directions – is eminently good and for two main reasons. First, the centenary of the academic discipline in 2019 provides excellent opportunities to look back and critically appraise the crossroads, the roads (not) taken, the frustrating dead ends and the advances (including fierce debates about what counts as an 'advance'). While the revisionist disciplinary historians contribute important knowledge about the past, scholars in the discipline generally display limited interest in History, including the history of the discipline itself, seeming to care most about their own small research gardens.[3] Second, the centenary also provides a good opportunity to look ahead, not least because scholars in the discipline somehow seem to lack a shared sense of direction currently. The three most recent decades have been characterized by a very significant expansion in the numbers of scholars, students, courses taught and research publications, as well as a significant widening of the scope of the discipline. While the numerical expansion is most welcome and presumably reflects an increased demand for specialized scientific knowledge about a globalized yet disorderly world, the widening of scope has left the discipline with an unnecessary identity crisis. What is the discipline? Who are we IR scholars? How do we define the boundaries of the discipline? Should there be any boundaries? In terms of numbers, the field was practised by a relatively limited number of scholars for large parts of the 20th century, and it would appear that the increase in the number of scholars has given rise to a diversity that has gone wild to some degree.[4]

The centenary milestone is crucially important, not only because it concerns foundational matters but also because of the (contested) symbolic and mythological functions of the year 1919. The book has its deliberate limits, focusing on the academic discipline of International Relations, not on international political thought throughout all known times or all sorts of thinking about the international (therefore a chapter is included on what a scientific discipline is).[5] I am fully aware of how the discipline did not emerge in 1919 or, for that matter and even more specifically, on the evening of 30 May 1919, which Ernst-Otto Czempiel (1965), among others, declares to be its date of birth. To suggest such a birth would be a performatively symbolic act or, as Martin Wight (1991) lectured 60 years ago, 'This is partly an illusion' (p. 5) or a myth (but we should then acknowledge that myths have their purposes and functions: see Barthes, 1957). In any case, the origin of the discipline was no single event; indeed, there were many origins and beginnings, just as a major river begins with smaller tributaries that eventually amount to a river. In this context, we must not forget that trajectories do not result from beginnings but rather from subsequent repetitions.[6] Nonetheless, in acceding to the symbolic 1919 birth of a discipline narrative, I find the following three observations compelling. First, in what was apparently the first book entitled *Theories of International Relations*, Frank M. Russell (1936) points out how two developments 'have finally pushed problems of international relations to the front and compelled attention to them' (p. 3): The industrial revolution expanding international interaction in the late 19th century (trade, communication and advances in military technologies) and 'the war'.[7] Second, the late 19th century was also characterized by the increased categorization of social science and humanities research/knowledge production within scientific disciplines. In this sense, the creation of IR as a scientific discipline represented the continuation of a broader trend. Third, on the basis of very extensive archival research, Jo-Anne Pemberton (2020; see also Knutsen, 2018) points out that it was the perception of the early practitioners of the emerging discipline that they had embarked on the process of creating 'the scientific study of international relations', and that they had done so for specified reasons (Ikeda, 2008; McCourt, 2017; Thakur et al, 2017).

The year 2019 is also important, particularly in relation to the objective of reconstructing our understanding of the discipline. In diagnosing the ills of the discipline, the book is reminiscent of Kal Holsti's (1985) *The Dividing Discipline*. In terms of an argument about the identity of a discipline, it also resembles E.H. Carr's (1961) *What is History?* What, then, is the 2019 issue? If attending numerous conference panels and workshops, and reading articles and books, count for something, then it seems to me that the following features characterize the state of current disciplinary affairs: IR has become an all-inclusive enterprise, for which reason many IR scholars have experienced a sense of identity loss. The discipline has become spineless, and its core has become unclear and contested *tous azimuth*. IR is occasionally called an asylum for scholars who feel unhappy in other disciplines for a variety reasons – indeed, unhappy

3

in disciplines per se. It is telling that a major professional association, BISA, will be convening its 2021 annual conference with the theme 'Forget International Studies?'.[8] Thereby the association invites us to continue a decades-long string of (contradictory) reflections on processes of forgetting and remembering IR as well as (some of) its practitioners (Bleiker, 1997; Rytövuori-Apunen, 2005; Wang 2007; Tickner, 2013; Owens, 2018).

This book is very much about processes of professional identity formation within (and outside) the IR discipline. I argue that the discipline currently finds itself in a present and real danger, and that this danger is to some degree paradoxically caused by its growth, success and freedom. Whereas the discipline, according to a self-image that is particularly widespread in the United States, is merely seen as a subset of political science, a subdiscipline, it is increasingly practised worldwide *beyond* political science and both within the social sciences *and* the humanities. The liberation from the prison of political science (Rosenberg, 2016) and other self-appointed master disciplines enables a diversity that would be unthinkable within the confines of the masters. The challenge therefore becomes to master the newly won freedom. The characteristics outlined here mirror profound changes in the sociology of the discipline, and in turn represent a present and real danger of 'IR' ending up as a floating or empty signifier. In this context, the widespread practice of reducing International Relations to just IR may in some cases symbolize more than merely a convenient technical abbreviation.[9]

Given that the project is to reconstruct our understanding of the discipline, which operational methodological procedures are available to us? The idea of using some of the available statistical data initially appears appealing. I am in favour of backing up arguments with statistical evidence, especially concerning issues where statistical data can be used to determine the validity of an argument. However, drawing exclusively on statistical data or existing quantitative studies would potentially *derail* the kind of project that this book represents. The problem is not that major parts of quantitative studies exist only, and for obvious reasons, where data are available or can be generated. Nor is the problem that this approach leaves key issues unexamined; that is, there is a lot of quantitative research on journal article metrics, considerably less on books, syllabi, professional associations and community data. The real problem is that, for the specific purposes of the present enquiry into the genesis and development of IR, including the discipline's key features, we are more in need of an *interpretation* of key terms than of quantitative studies that do not engage in conceptual explication and instead proceed in a key characterized by barefoot or anecdotal conceptualization. In other words, we must know the changing configuration of key understandings of the main *problematiques* of our discipline, which are spelled out over seven chapters.

As hinted at, the argument of this book is, in a nutshell, that an answer to the question 'What is International Relations?' takes more than sweeping generalizations, more than a study of just one country (Schmidt, 1998), more than empty references to 'the discipline' (Hobson, 2012), more than a focus on Anglo-American theorists (Smith, 1995) and more than statistics on 1,001 articles in five selected journals. It takes a wider focus than one on theory and on 'the west'. If this is the argument *ex negativo*, the positive version of the argument is that there is a (dynamic) discipline. It is defined by a (changing) set of questions, spans the social sciences *and* the humanities, has built a portfolio of theories (and theoretical traditions), is diverse and practised by a community of scholars throughout the world, hence it is a global discipline. In the following seven chapters, I elaborate the argument, assigning each of the chapters to an important dimension of discipline (see Figure 0.1, in which each outer circle represents an essentially contested concept).

As the discipline will be examined from seven different yet overlapping perspectives, there will inevitably be some repetition. One or more scholars will appear in several chapters, yet each time for different reasons. In designing this approach, I readily acknowledge that I took some inspiration from Laurence Durrell's series of novels *The Alexandria Quartet* (2012), in which Durrell narrates the story from four different perspectives. Just as Justine has her version of the story, so does each of the seven concepts in this book. It seems to me that such a multifaceted approach is a valuable alternative to sweeping generalizations based on shaky foundations. I hope it is also an alternative to giving up: see Ilan Zvi Baron's take on the task, "It is not that there is nothing called IR, far from it, but rather that attempts at defining its parameters, set out its limits, and identify its normal modes of research, are ultimately futile and are more akin to acts of simulation" (Baron 2015: 260).

Figure 0.1: Seven conceptual perspectives on International Relations

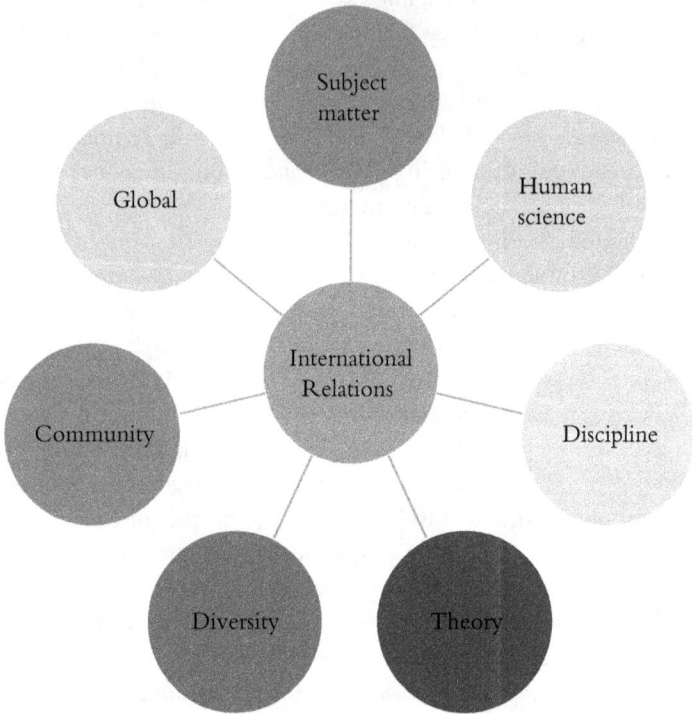

Source: Author

What is International Relations? is foremost an essay in which I try out a range of arguments in a tentative yet occasionally polemical fashion. It is one long argument in favour of the IR discipline, each chapter examining a key aspect of the general *problematique* (i.e. what is International Relations?). Each chapter outlines the main positions and suggests a path forward. In this structured and focused fashion, the not so hidden aim is to reframe how the discipline is understood, both within and possibly beyond the discipline itself. Given that the aim is also to provoke reflection, the book focuses on seven terms that are widely used and thus on key features of the discipline that are surprisingly rarely discussed. It follows that the chapter topics are about and are framed by essentially contested concepts: subject matter, discipline, human sciences, theory, diversity, community and global.

The seven concepts are eminently suited to challenge widespread groupthink in the IR community, including the various efforts to monopolize a certain meaning of a given concept. Given the complex nature of the concepts, they are also potentially capable of countering practices of shallow use, that is, assuming that their meaning is self-evident and thus not worthwhile explicating. Following W.B. Gallie's original coining of 'essentially contested concepts', they are here regarded as concepts that 'inevitably involve endless disputes about their proper uses on the part of their users' (Gallie, 1955: 169), and, moreover, it is the assumption that they apply foremost to 'philosophical and scholarly thinking' and therefore not to real-world politics (Gallie, 1955: 183; for a clear overview of Gallie's position and his critics, see Collier et al, 2006).[10]

Discipline is about subject matter, occasionally to such a degree that it is defined exclusively by its subject matter.[11] Chapter 1 describes how the issue of subject matter in IR is so controversial that it has triggered severe tensions and multiple identity crises. One side prefers a narrow subject matter, for instance, because it is seen as the most important of multiple, contending subject matters, or, more pragmatically, simply because it is seen as the feasible way forward. Other sides have other priorities or feel excluded from a narrowly defined discipline and therefore complain about the constraints of the discipline or call for an ever wider research agenda.[12] Mathias Albert and Barry Buzan (2017) are among the very few IR scholars who address the issue of subject matter in a slightly more structured and comprehensive fashion. Understandably, they are puzzled that a seemingly straightforward question – 'What is the subject matter of the discipline of International Relations?' – in IR 'is rarely addressed (let alone answered) in a direct fashion' (p. 898). In addition to examining the role of subject matter, Chapter 1 draws on Rudolf Stichweh's research on scientific disciplines and accordingly suggests downplaying the role of subject matter, recommending that we instead pay more attention to the questions asked by IR scholars. In turn, the chapter outlines the history of IR as a discipline defined by its guiding research questions.

Discipline is about being situated in the institutional environment of academic institutions. Chapter 2 highlights how IR was born into existing institutional and disciplinary settings. IR could therefore draw, yet also depended, on mental and institutional secessions from a wide range of existing disciplines (e.g. History, Law, Philosophy, Economics, Sociology) that were situated in the social sciences or the humanities. Subsequently, the discipline oscillated between these two big tents on university campuses, displaying profound variation across time and space.[13] In this context, Anne-Marie D'Aoust (2017) makes an excellent move, whereby she turns attention away from IR as a social science and towards the broader and more relevant issue: 'What kind of social science are we talking about?' This is a useful move because it enables a differentiation between different kinds of social science. One such kind is labelled 'American' by Stanley Hoffmann (1977), and another is represented by, among others, Alfred Schütz (1953/1962) and Peter Winch (1958/1990).[14] Winch comments on the unity of the sciences: 'I propose, in this monograph, to attack such a conception of the relation between the social studies, philosophy and the natural sciences' (p. 1).[15] In turn, the differentiation of the different kinds enables the social construction of the 'human sciences' category, that is, the outcome of a merger (or at least a shared mansion) of the social sciences and the humanities.

Discipline is about ... discipline. However, as an experienced scholar once noted, 'for a word so widely used, what constitutes a "discipline" is seldom discussed' (Wallerstein, 2000: 132). What is an academic discipline? How and when did disciplines emerge? How did they evolve? Does a preference for interdisciplinary research necessarily undermine disciplines? Why are IR's subdisciplines widely neglected? (And what are these subdisciplines anyway?) Chapter 3 explicates the nature of academic disciplines before subsequently embarking on an analysis of the trajectories characterizing the IR discipline. I also spell out the costs of abandoning disciplinary status and briefly examine possible alternatives. While the cons of disciplinarity have received generous coverage in the literature, thus becoming a veritable cottage industry, contributions seldom assess both the pros and the cons of disciplinarity, and very few examine the virtues of disciplinarity (Hunt, 1994; Maher, 2019). In this regard, Lynn Hunt is an admirable exception, who praises the virtues of disciplinarity.

Scientific disciplines are about theory (and theorizing), and therefore about yet another widely used yet difficult concept. As Raymond Aron (1967) observes, 'Few words are used as often by economists, sociologists, or political scientists as the word "theory". Few are as ambiguous' (p. 185). In conventional understandings, a discipline is defined by its subject matter *and/or* its theories and methodologies. Chapter 4 engages in a meta-theoretical analysis of the nature of theory and the theorizing processes. The chapter also explores the functions of theory, in terms not of its application in theory-informed empirical studies but for academic disciplines, including how scholars across time and space understand and value theory, such as theories developed in China (Kavalski 2014; Kim, 2016; Qin, 2018), the Middle East (al-Azm, 1981) or India (Mallavarapu, 2010). Finally, the chapter presents theories as question generators, a role that clearly connects to arguments made in Chapter 1.

Discipline is about diversity, and Chapter 5 explores the relationship between discipline and diversity. According to one perspective, the relationship should be seen in contradictory or mutually exclusive terms. Whereas supporters of diversity want less discipline, supporters of discipline consider diversity a threat to disciplinary coherence. My argument is that discipline and diversity can be mutually supportive and that, in multiple practices, the IR discipline is as diverse as it gets. The increasingly frequent calls for greater diversity and decentring are intriguingly at odds with the bemoaning of fragmentation, which is not quite a novelty but which for decades has been a constant in stocktaking studies (Kristensen, 2015).

The social construction and reproduction of disciplines would come to a full stop without communities of scholars to make disciplines viable (i.e. the living practices of knowledge production). We must therefore take a step back and ask: What is a community? Peter Hamilton (1998) observes that 'the concept of community has been one of the most compelling and attractive themes in modern social science, and at the same time one of the most elusive to define' (p. 7). He adds that the notion of community is 'apparently elegant but infuriatingly slippery' (Hamilton, 1985: 7).[16] Chapter 6 pays a visit to the community of scholars who are cultivating the IR garden, especially their symbols and values and, together with them, their capacity to construct a symbolic or imagined community that, for them, provides identity and meaning. They might consider their community an ideal, a reality or both. The chapter is thus about scholarly interaction, communication and professional associations. The chapter also includes a visit to the institutions that do not recognize IR as a discipline; indeed, hardly even as a field of study. Such institutions include UNESCO, the European Union (EU) and a number of national science bureaucracies, but also professional non-IR societies and associations (Martínez-Frías and Hochberg, 2007).

The discipline is about relations that are 'international' or 'global'.[17] However, what is international depends on the position of the observer, and observations may well be influenced by the space in which the observer is situated. Hans Morgenthau (1962) draws our attention to this issue, referring to *Standortgebundenheit*, a term he borrows from the famous sociologist Karl Mannheim. The observer-observation-perspective *problematique* is one of the prime reasons IR is so fascinating as well as so challenging. The argument I forward is that the discipline is indeed global and that 'globalizers' and 'parochials' share a neglect of the actually existing global nature of the discipline. Significantly, accounts of 'the discipline' often turn out to be nothing more than accounts concerning contributions in English or from the US or, more broadly, from 'the west'. In this context it is most fortunate that current efforts to globalize the discipline tend to destabilize long-held narratives about the origins and growth of the discipline over the course of the 20th century. The three factors – self-images, numbers and disciplinary globalization – combined are bound to have an impact on disciplinary identities. Ironically, calls for global diversity frequently turn out to praise practices of exclusion.

Finally, I should emphasize that I have no intention to engage in 'boundary work', or police demarcations, or to be the referee in determining who or what should be included or excluded. Attempting to do so might make a splash, but I prefer to go for a bigger splash by outlining updated settings for the discipline, thereby aiming to frame the conversation about the core of the discipline that we are bound to have. While there is no direction home, we should be able to identify something that is agreeable in the current predicament, thereby determining the core, the subdisciplines and what is (not) within the boundaries of IR as an academic discipline.

1

What is the Subject Matter?

Introduction

Subject matter matters in an almost existential fashion, not least because scholars conventionally insist on using it to define the discipline. Hence disciplines are frequently defined by the subject areas they cover and perhaps for good reasons. Think about it. Within a discipline, it intuitively seems justified to expect a common understanding of what is under the microscope. Nonetheless, the subject matter in IR is one of the most hotly contested issues. In the words of Michael Cox (2005), editor of *International Relations*: 'At a time when the discipline is split into ontological tribes who speak only to themselves, and in their own languages, it was refreshing to hear a scholar seeking to connect, even if the medium was "battle"' (p. 337). Cox's assessment is widely shared and, as Christine Sylvester (2013) adds, 'debate, once thought of as a disciplinary sport, is now mostly confined to within-camp issues' (p. 615).[1]

In the contested issue of subject matter, two main trends stand out: 'narrowers' versus 'wideners'. The two first sections of the chapter examine narrow and broad understandings of the subject matter. The challenge is not only that our answers to the question 'What's under the microscope?' evolve historically; that seems to apply to all scientific disciplines, and in the natural sciences it is one of the main premises of Thomas Kuhn's well-known idea about paradigms and paradigmatic shifts. By contrast, within the scientific study of international relations, the issue triggers not successive paradigm shifts but rather fundamental disagreement about what the discipline is and what it should be about. Indeed, social scientists triggered Kuhn's hunch about the significance of paradigms. He recalls how spending a year

> in a community composed predominantly of social scientists confronted me with unanticipated problems about the differences between such communities and those of the natural scientists among whom I had been trained. Particularly, I was struck by the number and extent of the overt disagreements between social scientists about the nature of legitimate scientific problems and methods. (Kuhn, 1962/1970: viii)

While the overt disagreements prompted Kuhn to begin to think in terms of paradigmatic shifts concerning material reality, it does not necessarily follow that his idea also applies to social reality. It is telling that Kuhn published his book as part of the *International Encyclopedia of Unified Science*, indicating that both author and editors believed in a unified science.

However, is it inevitable that debates about subject matter are dead ends? It is not. One can indeed argue that it is not the subject matter, but rather the questions asked, that defines disciplines, and this understanding is the topic of the third section. This third option, that is, the rejection of the dilemma, offers a way out of the impasse characterizing the debates on the stretching of subject areas, a debate in which the participants have been walking in circles for decades, repeating the same normative arguments about what the subject matter ought to be.

When the discipline is not defined by its subject matter or by the questions asked, it is often defined by its theories (see Chapter 4). A consequence of this close connection between discipline and theory is that many books pretend to be about the discipline but are really only about its theories. In any case, the move to theory only delays the moment when the subject matter kicks in. In this context and concerning the theory–subject matter nexus, Kenneth Waltz (2003) has pointed out an important precondition for theory building: 'First, in order to have a theory, you'll have to have a subject matter, because you can't have a theory about everything. There's no such thing as a theory about everything.'[2] In Chapter 4, we return to the dimension of theory. At this point, it is important to note the linkages between theory and subject matter.

Domaine réservé

Narrow understandings of the subject matter tend to see it as some kind of 'reserved domain', but there is a pronounced variation across time and space about exactly how narrow – and 'narrow how' (i.e. in which way narrow). Both issues are sufficiently contested to prompt occasional toxic controversies. Given that the discipline's research agenda is evolving or in flux, such variation should come as no surprise, nor should it cause too much concern. This chapter is therefore not about the many different definitions of subject matter but about how different definitions of subject matter have an impact on understandings of the discipline. The following examples show how conceptions of subject matter shape conceptions of discipline.

Historically, the International Studies Conferences (ISC), functioning under the auspices of the League of Nations, convened scholars in Europe and beyond who shared an interest in developing the study of international relations. Hence the conferences functioned as an important hub for the emerging discipline (Long, 2006; Riemens, 2011; Pemberton, 2020).[3] The main topics on the ISC agenda were – in addition to defining the scientific study of international relations – the role of the state in economic affairs, collective security and peaceful change. These topics reflected aspects of world politics at the time, and it is difficult to detect a cumulative effect on the genesis of the discipline. One might argue that the controversial issue of the responsibility for the First World War was also on the agenda, but it was more on the ISC's political agenda as opposed to the research agenda.[4] The relationship between diplomatic and scholarly activities was intimate, and many scholars actually had considerable experience of diplomacy, from direct or participatory observation. They *knew* the subject matter, and while they aspired to launch the scientific study of international relations, they saw no need to specify the subject matter.[5]

Holsti (1985) represents the view that the subject matter should be defined in a relatively narrow fashion; specifically, that IR's subject matter is about war and peace. He claims that there is a

300-year-long consensus about this and, worst of all, that this consensus is now broken. Holsti argues that, in moving away from a focus on the relations between states, IR has gone astray. However, the problem is not that theories are equated with the discipline or that the 300-year-long consensus has ended. The real problem for Holsti's consensus–disarray diagnosis, is that the consensus is an imagination that never existed. The theories of international relations in 1936, 50 years before Holsti wrote his book, were about a broad range of topics (Russell, 1936). IR was never only about war and peace but has always also been about sociological, normative, economic, religious, governance and technological affairs. It is telling that the first international organizations focused on postal services and telegraphed communication; not exactly the core business of peace and war. Thus, without a broken consensus, the disarray problem is left with one foundation less.

Holsti is far from alone in being state-centric or in only having an eye for peace and war. The original English School also had a predominantly narrow understanding of the subject, focusing on the international society of states and little else. It showed limited interest in features – such as economics, transnational interaction and regional integration – that transcended the international politics of states. Within the English School, it is members of the solidarist branch in particular who demonstrate an openness to a wider conception of the subject matter, whereas pluralists tend to lean towards a narrow conception, focusing on interstate relations.

In analytical terms, the subject matter can be conceptualized in terms of actors, structures and processes. Actors range from states (in state-centric studies) to a multitude of different kinds of actors. One example is John Ruggie's (2004) concept of the global public domain, populated and shaped by states, civil society organizations, international organizations and transnational corporations. Thus, Ruggie's global public domain includes the states system but also considerably more than that. Moreover, the non-state actors do not merely seek to influence the state-based system, aspiring instead to shape global politics directly by means of their own actions, aspirations that are occasionally successful.

In some cases, scholars define the subject matter in terms of material or social reality. Each option has profound consequences for the subject matter and, in turn, for conceptions of discipline.

In each case – material and social – scholars miss the other side of the coin, and the ensuing understanding of the discipline turns out to be an awkward scholastic discipline with self-inflicted limited capacity to produce insights about world affairs.

As an unintended or accidental consequence of the growth of the field (e.g. in the number of scholars, institutions and funding), the socialization of the new arrivals, whether people or institutions, was rather unsuccessful in reproducing the existing norms and rules of the discipline. One segment of scholars decided to abandon the discipline, despite simultaneously demanding recognition as scholars in the field, notably a field characterized by an unlimited conception of what the subject matter could be. They abandoned the discipline because they saw it as an unwarranted constraint. They viewed the discipline as fragmenting into pieces and applauded the process for one of two reasons. The first was that they regarded it as a self-contained discipline, cultivated mainly in the US and characterized by a state-centric focus, a priority given to defence–security *problematiques* and underpinned by narrow positivist conceptions of social science. The second was that they understood the general nature of disciplines in a Foucauldian fashion; that is, with an emphasis on regulation, sanctions and punishment (Ashley and Walker, 1990a; Grenier, 2015). No matter which reason, they regard the subject matter as narrow and prefer something much wider.

Both the 1960s and 1990s witnessed incursions of epistemology so strong that the subject matter almost disappeared. The guiding research question did not concern the actually existing actors, structures and processes but how we can know about these phenomena. Bull (1969) famously characterized behavioural studies as 'as remote from the subject of international politics as the inmates of a Victorian nunnery were from the study of sex' (p. 26). Whereas mainstream scholars shared characteristics with Bull's inmates of Victorian nunneries in terms of being remote from the study of sex, dissenters by contrast were almost obsessed with the study of sex, both their own and that of others.

The narrowest conception of subject matter is likely the one that turns out to be the author (i.e. narcissist self-reflective studies). In such cases, the subject matter is reduced to the dialectics of me–myself–I. The observer is king or queen in this conception and the world has disappeared, or perhaps it is reduced to being a canvas on which images of the self are painted. Self-reflective studies of this kind became relatively popular during the 1990s, especially within the parts of IR that take their cue from the humanities. Authors of self studies have limited interest in discipline except perhaps as a stepping stone or antithesis to their main interests. In such a context, it is unsurprising to encounter the argument that anyone can 'join' IR, regardless of whether their formal training was as economists, anthropologists or historians (Griffiths and O'Callaghan, 2001).

Finally, some might suggest that Stanley Hoffmann's (1977) famous article 'An American Social Science: International Relations' defines the subject matter of IR. However, social science is an organizational category, not a subject matter (see Chapter 2). Moreover, the act of defining the subject matter does not led to a distinct conclusion that IR is (not) a discipline. Whereas Holsti prefers a narrow focus and concludes that IR is not a discipline, Puchala (2003) believes that the focus should be considerably wider: 'Relations between states and peoples constitute a distinct realm of human activity' (p. 8); but he concludes that IR is a discipline, even a mature discipline.

Widening the subject matter: *tous azimuts?*

When the subject matter is defined in an extremely narrow fashion (e.g. as the self of the author), it is not difficult to become part of the wideners' camp. But that is also the case when mainstream scholars define the subject matter, as represented earlier by Holsti. Wideners typically argue that narrow understandings do not reflect the increasing complexity of world politics and economics, that the discipline should reflect complexity to remain relevant and that it therefore requires broader horizons. Calls to widen the subject matter and thereby the discipline have been on the agenda for half a century. One of the first important wideners of consequence was Susan Strange (1970), who urged the inclusion of international political economy (IPE), a move reaching back to former practices, for instance in the ISC (see also Ashworth, 2011b; Osiander 1998; de Wilde 1991).[6] She argues that it is crucially important to revive the IPE tradition, such as the politics of money, finance, transnational corporations and single commodities such as oil, copper and uranium. It was a very successful call, which was aided by developments in the global economy (oil crisis, economic crisis and the new prominence of transnational companies). IPE studies became a new cottage industry and the discipline a wider enterprise, equipped with a revived subdiscipline.

The revival of IPE overlapped with parallel efforts to go beyond interstate relations and to include transnational relations (Kaiser, 1969; Keohane and Nye, 1971, 1977, 1987). It was also a successful initiative, largely for the same reasons as the IPE initiative. In this context, it is relevant to include the focus on international organizations. While international organizations had been on the research agenda for decades and were thus part of research within the discipline, the focus on international regimes was an addition and a very popular subject during the 1980s, if not a fad that came and somewhat declined later. Cooperative arrangements also existed at the regional level, and processes involving cooperation and regional integration became part of the subject matter, and eventually led to the creation of the subdiscipline on regionalization. With processes of globalization and emerging patterns of global governance, the subdisciplines, on the one hand, represented fault-lines of subject matters and, on the other, enabled the arrival of joint-venture research programmes, such as bringing together sociological and social anthropological approaches.

By the end of the 20th century, the arrival of numerous additional subject matters rendered the discipline a much more pluralistic enterprise, and it is no exaggeration to say that IR entered the 21st century as a fundamentally transformed discipline, equipped with a broad range of subject matters and, not to forget, subdisciplines (see also Chapter 3). It had been transformed into a mature discipline, underpinned by solid foundations of meta-theoretical reflections and an emerging disciplinary historiography. Strictly speaking, these features are perhaps not part of the subject matter per se, but they are part of what it takes to be a mature discipline (Gunnell, 2018).

Contemporary trends are somewhat different. The discipline has been widely criticized for being too narrow, neglecting important issues, downplaying culture, race and/or gender, or not listening to voices that have been unheard or silenced. There have been widespread pleas to extend the research agenda to ever more subject matters, to transcend the Anthropocene focus which reduces the subject to human affairs, to think outside the box, and to understand the international, the world or the global in an unlimited fashion.

In short, to go *tous azimuts* in an unhinged fashion. As mentioned earlier, such criticisms are plenty and have been triggered by an array of factors. Heléne Pellerin (2012) eminently nails the impact of sociological change: 'The universal pretension of the discipline of International Relations (IR) is increasingly being questioned by scholars who feel that the theories and issues that IR deals with do not represent their views on history and current events' (p. 59). In some cases, the unease with inherited disciplinary views is translated into the rationale of books and recently launched book series. The *SAGE Handbook of the History, Philosophy and Sociology of International Relations* (Gofas et al, 2018) is deliberately pitched as representing a younger generation's perspective on IR, which is intended to be as much forward looking as a retrospective review of accomplishments, and which is informed by History, Philosophy and Sociology (HPS), two disciplines from the humanities and one from the social sciences. In this project, IR disappears as a discipline and morphs into an interdisciplinary field. Like HPS, Bristol Studies in International Theory (BSIT) aims to represent and encourage reflections by a new generation, but in contrast to HPS, it has an identity within IR as an academic discipline.

One of the BSIT editors, Felix Berenskoetter (2012), observes an oscillation between being within and going beyond IR:

> There is no lack of theorizing among junior scholars whose background and outlook is arguably less American than that of previous generations, and whose conceptual work draws on political theory, philosophy, sociology, history, psychology, religion, geography, media studies, literary studies, etc. – the list goes on. These creative endeavours offer fresh angles on world politics, its very conception, and how to study it. The question is, do the authors still identify with 'IR' as an intellectual home?

A research methods book addressing popular culture and international relations includes topics such as video games, art, music, movies, television series, advertising, memes, viral videos, comic books/graphic novels, literature and more (Caso and Hamilton, 2015). Such a broad collection of topics demonstrates that the contributors and, for instance, the founders of the English School live worlds apart. For the founders of the English School, including Martin Wight and Hedley Bull, the subject matter was states and their interaction in international society. In arguing against a narrow definition of the discipline, the editors of the volume, Federica Caso and Caitlin Hamilton, represent the contemporary Zeitgeist and are keen to create a nexus between popular culture and IR, thereby contributing to a new IR subdiscipline (on subdisciplines, see Chapter 3).

Chih-yu Shih and Jiwuy Yin (2013: 72), employ the term 'ontological incongruence' for global orders that constitute different types of units – states, civilizations or empires – and how these units are intertwined. Compared to the conventional state-centric approach, the inclusion of empires and civilizations marks a radical extension.[7] The conceptual triptych enables the inclusion of non-western IR theories, and thus a better understanding of the degree to which global IR theories reflect contemporary practices of global politics (see also Chapter 7). I argue that an ontology of parallel worlds helps us to better understand the dynamics of contemporary conceptualization and theory building in a discipline that is in a state of 'after hegemony' (Jørgensen, 2014; 2017a). However, ontological incongruence is not only about global orders constituted by different types of units and how these units are intertwined; it also concerns our specialized vocabularies.

No friend of discipline, Felix Grenier's (2015) understanding of IR as a discipline leads him to argue that the discipline has a restrictive impact:

> They restrict the diversity of actors, activities and ideas that can participate in IR ... they marginalize the plurality of actors, activities and ideas that currently contribute to IR thinking but that do not strictly conform to the dominant understanding of appropriate approaches to knowledge production, ontologies and applications in the field. (p. 251)

The problem is that he blames the discipline for something that only applies to a distinct version of it. It is the predominant practices within North American universities that prompt Grenier's resistance to restrictions (i.e. practices cultivating narrow methodological procedures), IR as a subset of political science and a neglect of what Grenier calls 'geo-epistemic diversity'. Thus, the main problem with Grenier's critique is that he generalizes the characteristics of a distinct version of the discipline, thereby neglecting the actually existing geo-epistemic diversity of a discipline in multifaceted colours.

Mathias Albert and Barry Buzan (2017) contribute one of the few and by far the most comprehensive examination of the discipline–subject matter nexus. Among the many subject matters on offer, they search for one capable of claiming the title of *primus inter pares*. This search leads them to considerations about the sources of identity formation, especially labels, intellectual traditions and methodology. Finally, they outline two distinct approaches: subject matter defined as *realm* and as *scale*. For each approach, they discuss the implications for the study of international relations. They conclude that, while each approach leads to a conception of the discipline that is different from the other approach, they share the feature of contributing to a platform on which it is possible to define the discipline in substantive terms. Albert and Buzan seem to offer the most advanced contribution to efforts to define the discipline in such terms. It is therefore time to leave the feature of subject matter and to proceed to considering an alternative.

Defined by its guiding research questions

Over the course of the last 100 years, the issue of subject matter drove processes of disciplinary identity formation, and crystallized in debates on defining the discipline. Such debates matter because scholars often use subject area to define disciplines. Debates between 'narrowers', 'wideners' and the ubiquitous pragmatic 'middle-of-the-roaders' have been a constant and can, in principle, continue endlessly. The previous sections have revealed how toxic and inconclusive such debates can be. The value added by these debates would therefore appear to diminish by every new article that is published on the topic. Importantly, other disciplines have been in a similar situation, yet have managed to change tack and move on to more productive endeavours. I believe it is time for IR to also change tack, hence the present section. It is based on the hunch that Richard Ned Lebow (2001) is onto something very important when he provocatively claims that 'ideas that propel science to the next stage of inquiry rarely grow out of existing research' (p. 116). While research on the general development of disciplines obviously also belongs to the category of existing research, it is conducted outside the echo chambers of IR and thereby outside increasingly unproductive scholarly path dependencies. The way forward cannot be increased narcissism. Hence I turn to research on scientific disciplines.

In his outline of the development of modern scientific disciplines, Rudolf Stichweh (1992) highlights a radical discontinuity in the historical development of disciplines, a discontinuity that 'legitimated the perception of autonomous individual scientific disciplines as being uncontrollable by outside forces' (pp. 7-8). In turn, he advances the following argument: 'From this point on, disciplines can be defined by *guiding research questions* rather than by subject areas. This radical transformation renders it difficult to conceive of the development of a discipline any longer as the cumulation of knowledge about its subject area' (Stichweh, 1992: 8). Stichweh is aware of how the guiding research questions that he suggests for the definition of a given discipline 'might resist any attempt to answer them definitely', for which reason the development of a discipline may be perceived as 'a sequence of tentative answers' (p. 8). In contrast to the non-cumulative production of knowledge about subject areas, the development of the sciences is cumulative. If new problems emerge, they often prompt the emergence of subdisciplines or new disciplines.

Unfortunately, we do not handle questions particularly adeptly. Lebow (2001) rightly points out that graduate training typically focuses on theory application and methodological procedures for arranging encounters between theory and evidence: 'little if any emphasis is placed on teaching students how to pose the questions that drive their research, or to ascertain why they are interesting' (p. 113). In this context it is indicative that books on research design are predominantly about analytical technicalities and not about the overall design of research projects.[8] Lebow also points out how Thomas Kuhn's paradigmatic shifts are really about the moments when a set of questions is replaced by a new set of questions. Finally, Lebow draws a distinction between small and big questions, suggesting that some branches of social science are better at answering small questions, whereas interpretivists are best at handling big questions. With this differentiation or division of labour, Lebow's approach is different from that of Charles Taylor: that the subject matter of the human sciences – human actions and social arrangements – always requires interpretation (Little, 2009; see also Adams et al, 2005; Little, 2016).[9]

In the following sections, I shall explore the significance of Stichweh's argument about disciplines being defined by their guiding research questions while remembering that definite answers should not be expected. I will briefly outline the main guiding questions that define the IR discipline and describe its development as a sequence of tentative answers. Thereby I deliberately move away from the discipline-defined-by-its-subject-matter approach. Moreover, Stichweh's approach seems incompatible with the image of a sequence of 'great debates', no matter whether or not scholars see these debates as representing epistemological progress. In short, this is an invitation to experimental thinking about the growth of the IR discipline. In order to keep the task within what is feasible in the present context, I shall focus on just a dozen guiding questions. There may well be more than a dozen, just as some will contest the selection of questions. What is also worth remembering is the distinction between the discipline and its numerous subdisciplines, not least the sets of guiding questions that define these categories of communication and knowledge production.

1. What are the causes of war and the conditions of peace?

The question is as classic as it gets, and it was on the mind of the members of the epistemic community who, convening during the Paris Peace Conference, thought it time to launch a scientific discipline of International Relations. The first tentative answers followed soon after, answers that specifically focused on the causes of the First World War, and, significantly, scholars in losing and winning countries tended to agree about the relevance of the question but disagreed about the answers.[10] The same thing happened after the Second World War, when Japanese scholars devoted themselves to searching for the causes of war and explaining what had gone wrong (Alagappa, 2011; Yamamoto, 2011). After the Cold War, Russian scholars asked the same question. In addition to these examples, research traditions offer tentative answers, for instance peace research, security studies and war studies. Helga Haftendorn (1991) and Jack Levy (1998) offer very useful overview of developments and advances in parts of the world.

2. What is international society?

The question has been on an eventful journey, beginning with the term 'international society' playing a role in discourses of diplomatic practice and subsequently entering public discourse only to end up in disciplinary reflections. Early tentative answers include those of Masamichi Royama (see Ikeda, 2008), Alfred Zimmern (1934) and Georg Schwarzenberger (1941). Charles Manning took it through a maturing process and presented the result as a tentative answer in *The Nature of International Society* (1962b). Subsequently, the question has been among those that have helped to boost the prominence of the English School and contributed to defining the discipline (Bull, 1977/1995; Jackson, 2000; Navari, 2021).

3. What is foreign policy?

Caught between the pillars of Political Science and International Relations, foreign policy studies faces the paradox of being rejected by both public policy studies and what some call 'proper' International Relations while being immensely popular with the IR community at the same time. In this context, it is important to stress that acknowledging the value of a distinction between international relations and foreign policy does not necessarily imply a narrow IR horizon that excludes foreign policy. Hence it seems to me that 'What is foreign policy?' is a research question that has been on the agenda throughout the discipline's existence; as one of its most popular subdisciplines, it is nothing less than co-constitutive of the discipline. Indeed, what would international relations be without states' foreign policies and what would IR be without the subdiscipline and its specialized journals?

4. What is power politics?

It was questions about power and politics that helped create demarcation lines between international law and the emerging

IR discipline. As E.H. Carr writes, 'In the first place, *The Twenty Years' Crisis* was written with the deliberate aim of counteracting the glaring and dangerous defect of nearly all thinking, both academic and popular, about international politics in English-speaking countries from 1919 to 1939 – the almost total neglect of the factor of power' (Carr, 1939/1946: vii). Carr was far from alone in this analysis. Indeed, the next three decades demonstrated an explosion of interest in the features of power and the related term 'power politics' (e.g. Schwarzenberger, 1941; Wight, 1946; Morgenthau, 1948). The Second World War did not continue to provide real-world events to feed the continued relevance of the question, yet the Cold War was eminent in doing so for the next 40 years. Given that this period was also the decades when the IR discipline became consolidated, the question about power politics had more impact on defining the discipline than it might otherwise have done (Vasquez 1998; Mearsheimer 2001).

5. What is the international system?

Over time, the question about the nature of the international system triggered a sequence of tentative answers. At the time Kenneth Waltz (1959) published his political theory treatise *Man, the State and War*, and carved out explanations for systemic theories, the behavioural revolution was underway; though it was mainly focused on domestic political systems, it had a not negligible impact on the study of international relations (Kaplan, 1957). The two contending perspectives – Waltz versus Kaplan – have each triggered a whole range of associated questions, including structural features, configurations of polarity, power politics, factors triggering conflict, development, the arms race, game theory and so on. It is only more recently that additional perspectives and accompanying answers have emerged, including applied systems theory (Jervis, 1998) and Niklas Luhmann's sociological systems theory.

6. What is IR theory?

It will soon be 90 years since the question began to be asked, and the trajectory of tentative answers show many swings and turns.

During the interwar years, a few scholars did employ the term 'theory' but it was almost entirely synonymous with international thought (Russell, 1936). During the 1950s and 1960s answers branched out in different directions. While international thought continued to qualify as theory, there was a parallel movement aimed at parcelling out a narrow social science understanding of theory, which reserved the concept for explanatory theory, thus excluding normative and interpretive theory. In terms of substance, it is easy to detect a trend towards a much wider repertoire than the two-school approach (Liberalism versus Realism). The portfolio of tentative answers might be described as rich and dispersed but that does not mean that the question is not one of the most important guiding questions that help define the discipline.

7. What is the relationship between international politics and economics?

The question figures high on the agenda and the sequence of tentative answers confirms its prominence. Given its formative phase took place in the wake of the global financial crisis in the 1930s, it is not surprising that IR scholars placed IPE high on the research agenda (Osiander 1998; Ashworth 2011a). The diverse answers to the question also show how the fundamental question leads to more specific propositions, for instance those associated with theories of imperialism and commerce liberal theory. Later additions, such as a *dependencia* theory and theories of globalization confirm the diverse directions IR studies can take. Regardless of the approach taken by scholars on these questions, the answers remain tentative.

8. What is international organization?

While the question drives a thriving subdiscipline on global governance today, it used to focus almost entirely on the League of Nations. The league and the few functional agencies from the late 19th century constituted the 'institutional turn', and made it meaningful to wonder about the impact the turn might have on international affairs and on the role of states in international society. Several books provide excellent overviews of the scholarship on the issue and together offer fascinating tentative answers to the question (Kratochwil and Mansfield, 2005; Weiss and Wilkinson, 2013). It is telling for the dynamic character of the subdiscipline that the question about international organization at some point morphed into studies of global governance, a subdiscipline that also has its own specialized journals.

9. What is the relationship between power and morality?

Given that philosophy/political theory is part of the discipline's foundation, it is not surprising that one of the key research questions concerns the relationship between power and morality. Again, the answers are suggestive. What is perhaps surprising is that studies of the issue at times and places have been pushed to the margin of the discipline. What is also surprising is that such a claim is still valid if we widen the question to include ethics, norms and principles, that is, the entire normative superstructure. While the enforced 40 years' detour of normative theory (Giesen, 1992; Smith, 1992) is difficult to explain, there are various categories of answers to the question. Some claim that we face a zero-sum game, that is, either power or morality wins; others claim that power and responsibility cannot be separated; still others claim that power can be employed to achieve normative objectives.

10. What is community?

Steve Smith is among those who point to the significance of the questions asked. According to Smith (2008), the big questions that should animate scholarship should relate to:

> identity and how it relates to material interests; how identities are constructed; how they relate to patterns of political, economic, and social power, both between and within societies. How do we categorize our thinking? How do we construct the inside and the outside, or the public and the private realms, and therefore how do we develop the categories within which we 'do' international relations? (p. 781)

11. What is the role of culture, gender and race in international relations?

The question is one of several that are not being asked, or are being asked only relatively late in the discipline's development or only in some places. While culture made some inroads during the early years of the discipline in the form of studies of civilization, its role was limited to specific aspects such as diplomatic culture, strategic culture, organizational culture and political culture, the latter typically entering the analysis in second-image explanations of (changing) foreign policy directions. While gender has obviously always been present in international relations and thus an implicit part of the ten previous questions, it took 60 years to appear on IR's radar as an explicit research question that contributed to define the discipline, at least in some parts of the world. Gender appeared on the radar at about the same time, whether or not accidentally, as the brief interest in class declined. Questions about race appeared even later, though there are tentative statements that race was among the discipline's foundational cornerstones, at least in (western) parts of the world (Hobson, 2012; Vitalis, 2005, 2015; Thakur et al, 2017).

12. What is a scientific discipline?

The twelfth and final guiding research question in the list of master questions is about the IR discipline, our discipline. Though it is often ridiculed by empiricists as navel-gazing exercises or academic inbreeding which do not contribute to knowledge about global affairs, critical self-reflective studies should be recognized and appreciated as a natural part of mature disciplines. Fortunately, the question 'What is IR?' has been and continues to be a constant defining research question, to which a sequence of tentative answers have been offered. The research question entered the agenda during the interwar years, when it was phrased as 'What could an IR discipline possibly be?' As E.H. Carr put it, 'The science of international politics came into being in response to a popular demand. It was created to serve a purpose and has, in this respect, followed the pattern of other sciences' (Carr, 1939/1946: 2). The idea of a scientific discipline was born, and tentative answers were offered and debated throughout the world. However, in parts of the world that were under fascist or communist rule universities were not autonomous and disciplines were meant to serve the state. In other countries there were very few or no universities and therefore no scientific disciplines. A comprehensive account of the tentative answers to the question goes beyond the scope of this chapter but the book is intended as a contribution to such an account.

Conclusion

Scholars – past and present and probably also future – devote much energy to carving out a subject matter that is distinct for IR, and subsequently spend even more time in conversations about why *their* distinct slice is the best of all slices. The exercise is so popular that literally every decade yields numerous examples of the conclusion that there is no consensus. For a discipline that is exclusively concerned with material reality – such as physics – such an outcome would be a serious challenge and perhaps provoke a paradigm shift. Yet for a discipline such as IR, which is concerned with an ontology that includes both material and social reality, it is a rather predictable predicament. We have to live with it and, if possible, turn the inevitable into an advantage.

Changing perspective from subject area to questions asked does not imply that subject matter becomes irrelevant. Rather than being a tool used to define the field, subject matter becomes flexible and is derived from the questions. New problems trigger new questions, which can be dealt with within the discipline, in a subdiscipline or even outside the discipline. I subscribe to Felix Berenskoetter's (2012) assessment of 'isms':

> The theoretical traditions or 'isms' are not closed, static paradigms with clear arguments set in stone. Everyone who has ever tried to comprehensively survey an 'ism' knows they are diverse and highly dynamic bodies of thought. This is a different way of saying that 'boxing' individuals, schools, strands and tradition might be heuristically useful but also exceptionally harmful to actually existing diversity.

Moreover, I think Ferguson (2015) is (partly) correct in observing how IR 'is constantly being renovated and even drastically remodelled. IR is slowly but surely moving away from what once was an almost exclusive focus on states and interstate relations, rational decision making, the West, and white males' (p. 9). But Ferguson is only partly correct, and his conclusion seems more catchy and convenient than compelling. It seems to be based on the assumption that in western disciplinary matters the west has been and is the only show in town, as if non-western scholarship does not exist. Likewise, with his reference to 'white males', Ferguson fails to take into account contributions by males and females who are not white.[11] Moreover, IR may well be moving away from the west with increasing global diversity in the discipline, but teaching, research, and international policy (TRIP) survey data (Wemheuer-Vogelaar et al, 2016) suggest that global IR remains focused on states and interstate relations, rational decision making, and notions of civilization and empire, with both concepts often playing a prescriptive role (see also Chapter 7).

2

What are the Human Sciences?

Introduction

The contrast could not be starker between arguing, on the one hand, that IR is 'an American social science' (Hoffmann, 1977; see also Grosser, 1956), thus reducing IR to no more than a distinct social science in America, and, on the other hand, that IR is a 'craft discipline' (Jackson, 2000) or, according to Michael Donelan (1978), that 'the data of the human sciences are the product of thought. The study of international relations is the study of international thought' (p. 11). Subsequent contributions demonstrate that the issue remains high on the discipline's agenda (Alker, 1996; Brown, 2014; Neumann, 2014; D'Aoust, 2017).[1]

In this chapter, I argue that IR has always straddled or at least been at the boundary between the social sciences (e.g. Law, Sociology, Economics, Political Science) and the humanities (e.g. History, Anthropology, Literary Studies, Philosophy). Hence the chapter intervenes in debates about the inherent tension between the proponents of too little/too much (social) science and too much/too little humanities. Each position on the spectrum comes with important ideas about specified kinds of subject matter (see Chapter 1), as well as preferred theories and methodologies. This chapter spells out the ramifications of taking distinct positions and proposes that it is time to leave either/or options behind and instead acknowledge the human sciences as IR's heterogeneous home, that is, the wider camp spanning the social sciences *and* the

Figure 2.1: Constructing a heterogeneous hybrid field by
integrating the social sciences and the humanities

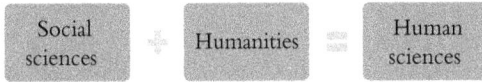

Source: Author

humanities (see Figure 2.1). Whereas the 'social' and the 'human'
aspects of the disciplines seem to get along or even be synonymous,
the 'science' part invites trouble not least because postmodern and
poststructuralist scholarship has spent the last 50 years admonishing
'science'. In other words, we are here at a crossroad and only some
will decide to take the road chosen in this book, that is, opt for IR
as a human science and using, for instance, Peter Winch as a tour
guide (Winch, 1958/1990; Hutchinson et al, 2016).

In professional practices, IR has always been a highly diverse
and pluralist undertaking (see also Chapter 5), and processes
of professional identity formation can draw on the differences
between and the similarities shared by the social sciences and the
humanities. However, straddling can be an uncomfortable position,
and some also feel that it does not qualify as a comfortable home.
Numerous attempts have been made to reduce IR so that it can
be at home exclusively within the social sciences, thus abandoning
the humanities; and there have also been attempts to push political
philosophy out of Political Science (see Ball, 1995; Puchala, 2003;
Burawoy et al, 2005). Such manoeuvring for position also works
in the opposite direction, and attempts at abandoning social science
are not at all uncommon, as seen in postmodern assaults on science
and poststructuralist procedures for critique and the deconstruction
of IR's scientific credentials (Jarvis, 2000; Holsti, 2001).

It is probably indicative of something that there is an intriguing
lack of balance between those who explore IR as a social science and
those who consider IR as a discipline within the humanities. While
an interest in the former generates considerable engagement, there
are strikingly few reflections on the latter. To make the argument
that IR should be seen as one of the human sciences, I begin by
examining IR as a social science, then look at how IR is practised
within the humanities, and finally outline how IR can be seen as
one of the human sciences.

IR as a social science

If we consider the discipline's multiple historical origins and beginnings, it was hardly its destiny to be considered exclusively as a social science. The broad variety of scholars who convened during the interwar years – to promote what they called an 'international mind'[2] and practical solutions to urgent practical problems as well as the study of international relations – came from all sorts of backgrounds. Their vision included the social sciences but also valuable insights from the humanities, reflecting their home in, for example, History or Philosophy. Nonetheless, many contemporary scholars consider the discipline's identity as a social science as a given, occasionally a reified given that is beyond question. In contrast, this chapter is based on the idea that this identity is not at all a given and, moreover and importantly, that there is considerable flexibility as to what it actually means to be a social science. In this context, it is significant that Patrick Jackson (2010) claims that all four ideal-type philosophical wagers should be considered social science.

While contributions from the 1930s and 1940s shared the aspiration to create a science about international relations, they provided limited specification of what exactly that would entail. Beyond the endeavour to define the scientific study of international relations, the debates at the ISCs were inconclusive (Amstrup, 1989; Pemberton, 2020). To understand contemporary images of the discipline, we must go back to the late 1940s and the impact of distinct (American) conceptions of social science. The developments in the US in the 1950s and 1960s that Hoffmann (1977) characterizes were (successful) attempts at reducing social science to an *American* social science underpinned by positivism, tasked with building empirical theories and making use of quantitative methodologies (Rosenau and Durfee, 1995; King et al, 1994; van Evera, 1997).[3] For IR made in the US during the 1950s and 1960s, the image of an onion or of a Russian matryoshka doll comes to mind: IR situated *within* Political Science, itself situated *within* the social sciences, although a social science painted in the stark positivist colours of the Vienna Circle philosophers.

By the early 1960s, two philosophies of the social sciences competed for the identity – if not the very soul – of social science: on the one hand, Peter Winch's (1958/1990) Wittgenstein-inspired philosophy of social science and, on the other, Vienna Circle philosophy applied

Figure 2.2: The 1950s and 1960s vintage version of US International Relations

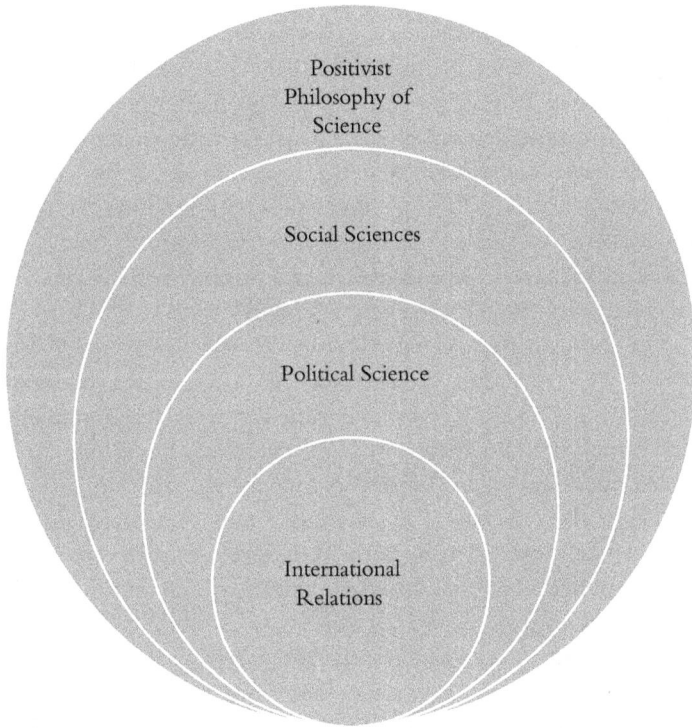

Positivist
Philosophy of
Science

Social Sciences

Political Science

International
Relations

Source: Author

to the social sciences (see e.g. Nagel, 1961; Braybrooke, 1965, a book prompted by Winch's book). One of the reasons the English School tends not to be understood among US scholars with a social science upbringing (e.g. Martha Finnemore, Dale Copeland, Robert Keohane) is that the English School leans towards the humanities. In this context, it is significant that Robert Jackson (2000) insists on the English School being a craft, not a science.

While there were scattered attempts around the world to copy the experiment in the US, they were less the rule and more exceptions to it. The American social science was an influential, well-funded experiment in one part of the world but no more than that. Moreover, the experiment often resulted in failure: it might have been grandiose, but nonetheless it failed (for an account of IR and foreign policy analysis failures, see Holsti, 1971; Carlsnaes, 2015). In short, in the US–American part of the world, social science may often be defined in universal terms, but it really just occupies one or two of the 81 quadrants of a full chess game of social science around the world. Yet the numerous failures of research programmes that are based on such narrow understandings of social science have not discouraged proponents; they merely try harder next time, always equipped with a righteous attitude. In all fairness, I should add that it is of little comfort that other conceptions of social science were equally unsuccessful in creating a healthy platform for a thriving discipline.

The social sciences camp is full of the little games academics love to play, including games about the status of IR. There are narratives about IR being either torn between 'real' disciplines or connecting the specialized yet parochial disciplines (e.g. Economics, History or Politics). Narratives on connecting would highlight the capacity of IR to analyse not the individual trees but the wood, including its trees. In IR terms, this is a capacity to analyse both the international society and the individual members of this exclusive society. It is quite easy to outline a narrative about IR being a helpless creature, torn between the real centres of the social sciences. When it is successfully pulled towards one of the centres, IR will be equipped with the main features of the pulling discipline. In such a narrative, IR can for instance be a subdiscipline of Political Science or a field of study applying the theories and methods of Economics (Cohen, 2007; Ashworth, 2011b).[4] Whatever the specifics of the narrative, it is ideal to tear apart images of IR as a discipline in its own right. Likewise, the last 30 years can be interpreted as a fight between rationalism and constructivism, or, in disciplinary language, between Economics and Sociology. It is easy to (unfairly) conclude that IR, presented as a creature helplessly bobbing about, is essentially an import business, a failed intellectual project that consumes the insights of genuine disciplines but is never capable of producing insights that scholars outside IR find interesting or relevant (Buzan and Little, 2001). The conclusion can also be flipped, in the sense that the discipline finds inspiration in its temporal, geographical and intellectual settings, and is capable of turning sources of inspiration into genuine and distinct knowledge about phenomena that other disciplines hardly care about.[5]

The unworthy-of-attention narrative about IR can also point to second-image explanations that do not disturb too much the bounded rationality of research on activities within bounded communities. Instead, explanations can rely on research on domestic features and merely add the international projection factor. In contrast, third-image explanations about the international, regional or global environment influencing domestic processes and institutions are a most subversive idea for parochial disciplines with reified national boundaries. Entire categories of social practices are no-go zones for these disciplines, which means no research is carried out on invasions or interventions. Despite the historical disappearance of principalities, kingdoms and states, there is limited research on the survival of political entities. Similarly, it is best to ignore the processes of globalization. Likewise, scholars doing research on party politics, social capital and econometrics seldom engage in research on genocides or the chemical weapons taboo.

The alternative narrative of the IR discipline connecting the parochial specializations is a road less taken. It is deeply puzzling that this road is not taken more often – would it not be joyful to point out the parochial nature of other disciplines and possibly even more joyful to offer all the missing links of which the parochials are unaware?

The literature on IR as a social science often turns out to be not about social science but about the *philosophy* of social science, or it addresses very general questions, such as the evergreen of whether IR is a science. In contrast, few studies display any interest in explicating exactly what being a social science entails, including the very different ideas about what a social science is or should be, or what goes on in the world of the social sciences, such as interactions between the different disciplines that make up social science.[6] This neglect is most unfortunate because it does not enable a structured debate that goes beyond the domain of assumptions, axioms if not prejudices about the contributions and linkages between distinct disciplines. The growing literature indicates a sustained interest in the issue, and both classical (Hoffmann, 1977) and contemporary contributions (Neumann, 2014; D'Aoust, 2017) engage with it in a comprehensive and innovative fashion.

IR has always managed to draw on some of the classical disciplines within the humanities, which is also why it has parts of their DNA in its intellectual genes. History, Philosophy and Anthropology played an important role in the genesis of IR, for which reason an IR without their impact would end up being a rump discipline. To understand the benefits (and costs) of a broadly conceived and inclusive discipline, we must travel to the world of the humanities.

With IR *chez Humanités*

When IR was gradually constituted as a discipline, half of the inspiration came from the humanities not least History and Philosophy. The interesting issue is therefore not only why the humanities continue to exert a pull of attraction, but also how these sources have experienced ups and downs, why they were abandoned by autarchic social scientists and how the humanities regained their prominence. In this context, two factors seem particularly important: constants and turns. The constants include History and Philosophy, while the major turns were the interpretive, cultural and linguistic turns.

With a focus on History, the drawing board is open to all sorts of adjectives, each designating a (sub)field of study or a subdiscipline. One example, diplomatic history, which was such a field and continues to be so. It may not always have been considered avant-garde or fashionable, but some of the premier studies in the discipline have emerged from the diplomatic history tradition. A second example is conceptual history, right from Reinhart Koselleck's pioneering work to Michael Freeden's work on conceptual analysis (Marjanen, 2017; Freeden, 2021). A third example is intellectual history and its connecting points to the history of IR theorizing (Bell 2001; Armitage, 2004, 2012; Hall, 2014; Vergerio, 2019; Navari, 2021). International organizations, with more than 100 years of history, is the subject of historical studies that often transcends the fairly narrow, functionalist studies within IR. Finally, some had great hopes and proposed the scientific study of international relations (Carr, 1939/1946), only to be disappointed and to move back to their original home in History; such was the case of E.H. Carr with the history of the Soviet Union.

On its own, Philosophy tends to forget international dimensions and issues, as inadvertently demonstrated by John Rawls' (1971) celebrated *A Theory of Justice*. Nonetheless, philosophy is an indispensable dimension of theorizing. Stefano Guzzini (2007: 23–4) highlights how theorizing comprises reflections on the conceptual, meta-theoretical and philosophical levels. Such reflections are as close to basic research as it gets, involving ontological and epistemological issues, together with conceptual work that draws on traditions of conceptual history and therefore transcending more simple explications of conceptual choices. Attempts to skip these levels of theorizing will result in more shallow studies and, collectively, in a less mature discipline.

'He was such an Arts man.' Anyone who has read Michael Nicholson's (1981) 'The Enigma of Martin Wight' will have noticed how he characterizes Wight. An intellectual lighthouse during the 1950s and 1960s, Wight extended the two-school IR discipline with an English School (Wight, 1991), contributed studies in diplomatic history and was among the first in the UK to outline a European Studies programme, acknowledging that Europe had become a region of the world, a significant change that called for a regional studies approach in the humanities (Wight, 1964). In combination, these were very neat accomplishments for an 'Arts man' in a discipline many considered to be merely a social science.

The main vehicles for the return of the humanities to IR are three theoretical turns.[7] The *interpretive* turn extended the portfolio of theory types. Whereas the hard or narrow-minded social science model only acknowledges explanatory theory, both interpretive and normative theory were brought back in, resulting in a revival of political theory (Ball, 1995), and within IR the (re-) emergence of the tradition of international political theory (IPT). The interpretive turn also included critiques of behaviouralism and rationalist templates (Taylor, 1971; Kratochwil and Ruggie, 1986). The *linguistic* turn drew on Continental philosophy, such as Wittgenstein's language games (Fierke, 2010) and speech act theory (Austin, 1962; Searle, 1969). While the linguistic turn produces multiple novel and insightful studies, it also has a dark side. John Lynn (1997; see also Lynn 2001) points out one such dark side:

> Concepts generated by literary and linguistic scholars
> seem particularly embarrassing in the study of history
> because they undermine the value of evidence and

> conclude that documents cannot actually tell us about
> reality but only about the author of the document. This
> 'linguistic turn' may be fine when approaching a novel
> or a poem, but it is usually malarkey when applied to
> the war archives. (p. 779)

Finally, the *cultural* turn extended the subject matter to the domain
of culture, a domain IR had largely neglected for decades (Lapid and
Kratochwil, 1996; for an exception, see Bozeman, 1960), although
individual contributions did offer reflections on, for instance, the
national character of states and the impact of (aristocratic) culture
on international diplomacy and international society (Cohen, 1997).
The cultural turn touches the bare bones of the key question of the
present book: 'What is International Relations?' Is it about interstate
relations or, as Bozeman (1960) advocated, is it about intercultural
relations, a field for which disciplines within the humanities, she
insisted, have significantly more to offer than disciplines within the
social sciences (for general overviews, see Valbjørn, 2006; 2008).

The humanities have their own dead ends, similar to the
destructive effects of positivism and behaviouralism in the social
sciences. Both postmodernism and poststructuralism contribute
to giving the third debate a bad name.[8] Once celebrated as
a source of diversity (and rightly so), the third debate has
demonstrated its own version of the dialectics of enlightenment.
Darryl Jarvis (2000) aims 'to expose the politics of postmodern
theory in International Relations whereby certain varieties of
postmodernist scholarship [in the broader social sciences] have
been plundered and pillaged of particular motifs, imported into
International Relations, and used in the pursuit of political ends'
(p. x). Examples include scholars who go bananas for orientalism
(as well as Eurocentrism), and who issue fatwas on mainstream
scholars with alarming frequency. Ironically, it is at the same time
difficult to detect much 'Said effect' in the social science-leaning
Middle East Studies (Valbjørn, 2008).

IR as a human science

In 2003 Donald Puchala highlighted Max Weber's intervention in
the *Methodenstreit* 100 years earlier, and his efforts to integrate two

camps, positivists and idealists (at the time called objectivists and historicists). As indicated by the chapter title ('Beyond the Divided Discipline'), Puchala is attempting to reach an integrated common vision of IR's identity. This chapter is informed by a similar idea, specifically, the idea to situate IR in the wider camp, which I refer to as the human sciences for lack of a better term, spanning the social sciences and the humanities. The former includes Law, Economics, Sociology and Political Science, and the latter History, Anthropology and Philosophy. Unfortunately, the existing literature reflects that most energy is devoted to pointing out the differences between the social sciences and the humanities. It seems to me that if one of these pillars were to win the task of designing IR, it would turn into a discipline that is unable to reach its full potential. Instead of building barriers between the two kinds of science, I seek to identify the value of each and to explore ways to combine them fruitfully. In the rest of this chapter, I therefore examine the ways in which IR would thrive under the umbrella of the human sciences.

The philosophical platform for such an integrated conception of the human sciences includes three highly prominent contributions. The first is Charles Taylor's (1971) essay 'Interpretation and the Sciences of Man', a sweeping critique of the behavioural revolution and the ways, which Taylor found unwarranted, in which it contributed to redesigning the social sciences.[9] Second, with *The Conduct of Inquiry in International Relations: Philosophy of Science and Its Implications for the Study of World Politics*, Patrick Thaddeus Jackson (2010) contributes to bringing back Max Weber to social science, a radical move in the US and elsewhere, where the social sciences have been understood in a very narrow fashion. With his intervention, Jackson aims at a new, or revived, balance between explanatory and interpretive approaches. Third, with *The SAGE Handbook of the History, Philosophy and Sociology of International Relations*, Gofas et al (2018) pay equal attention to sociology and philosophy, and as a more future oriented than a retrospective project.

IR's straddling of two of the main branches of the tree of sciences makes reflexive research on boundaries and contending perspectives a rewarding enterprise. Colin Elman and Miriam Elman (2008; see also Kennedy-Pipe, 2000) and their contributors examine how processes of professional socialization have a deep impact on how historians and IR scholars understand selected phenomena very differently. One of the main values of their book is that it does not remain at a general level, but demonstrates instead in very specific terms and citing distinct cases how certain topics are likely to be chosen (or neglected) for research, and how a historian and an IR scholar will each approach a topic, and then study it and, finally, draw conclusions. The book suggests that disciplinary perspectives are often more complementary than competitive. In other words, History scholars and IR scholars do not necessarily ask the same questions. They draw on different sources of evidence and hence, unsurprisingly, draw different conclusions. Importantly, this does not diminish the value of either of the two disciplinary approaches.

Numerous subdisciplines span the social sciences and the humanities. Historical sociology is a prominent example of a cross-over, making a priority of both historical and sociological dimensions. Notably, in recent years, historical sociology has enjoyed a surge, thus contributing to an IR under the auspices of the human sciences. The rise of historical sociology represents to some extent a return to the earlier prominent status of historical sociology, promoted by several French scholars, including young Stanley Hoffmann. Moreover, the philosophy of the social sciences is both an expression and a dynamic field of study. It is also an example of the idea that the social sciences, regardless of how they are defined, need anchors within the humanities. Similarly, IPT tends to span the social sciences and the humanities. Finally, the English School straddles the social sciences and the humanities, Bull and Buzan being more at home in the former and Wight and Watson in the latter. This bridge-building, hybrid nature of the English School is difficult to comprehend for scholars who are trained in a distinct and narrow social science tradition (Finnemore, 2001; Copeland, 2003). A genuine interest in inter- or multidisciplinary empirical research need not be anti-disciplinary, as it can be conducted on the basis of mutual recognition.[10] In short, plenty cross-overs exist, are practised and contribute to connecting two of the main branches of the sciences.

Being at home in the human sciences has consequences for any discipline, IR included. History becomes an indispensable beacon. While Hedley Bull dismisses the idea that History is simply the best at understanding international relations, he is also very clear on the significance of historical dimensions. Similarly, Puchala (2003) explores the relationship between History and IR precisely because he believes a non-relationship would be to the disadvantage of both disciplines. By contrast, bland scientism and ahistorical structuralism share the idea that historical dimensions can and should be dismissed. Dreams about realism as nothing less than timeless wisdom are so obsessed with continuity that historical change becomes inconceivable.

The way forward? Well, working towards coexistence, perhaps even mutual recognition, will be a highly challenging process for three reasons. First, centrifugal forces on all sides will continue to try to spoil the integrative project, meaning that the grand inclusion project might need to develop its own efforts at the active exclusion of destroyers. Second, socialization and specialization processes are bound to produce not only contending perspectives but also a lack of interest in what happens on the other side of the fence. If there is an interest, what scholars see is not necessarily valued in identical ways. Thus, Puchala points to the very different reviews that Adda Bozeman (1960) received when she published *Politics and Culture in International History*, ranging from the *American Political Science Review* being exceptionally negative to Harold Lasswell praising her great study. Yet this is just one of many cases of different criteria producing different evaluations and contributing to disintegrative efforts.

Meta-theoretical enquiries can help the project by pointing to shared underpinnings of otherwise contending perspectives. Within IR, for instance, Joseph Nye (1988) was among the first to quickly spot the shared underpinnings of neorealism and neoliberalism, underpinnings that greatly enabled the emerging neo-neo synthesis. Similarly, James March and Johan Olsen's (1988) analysis of the presence of functionalism in institutional studies is immensely helpful in understanding the fault-lines within not only the field they examine but also within IR institutional approaches. This explains why it is so rewarding to read Keohane's neoliberal institutionalist perspective through the lenses offered by March and Olsen.

From sociology of knowledge studies, we know that the red brick universities in the UK were once upon a time 'revolutionary' universities that broke with disciplinary traditions and provided space for IR, which at the time was a relatively new discipline, represented at a limited number of university campuses. Sussex University was such an experiment, testing *The Idea of a New University* (Daiches, 1964).[11] The case of red brick universities provides at least two insights: (1) in some parts of the world, there are no red brick universities and (yet) IR has not been liberated from its parent disciplines; (2) the promotion of IR as a human science will most likely happen in a piecemeal fashion and will depend on both genuinely reflexive dialogues and organizational change.

Figure 2.3: Building International Relations as a global human science (examples of building blocks)

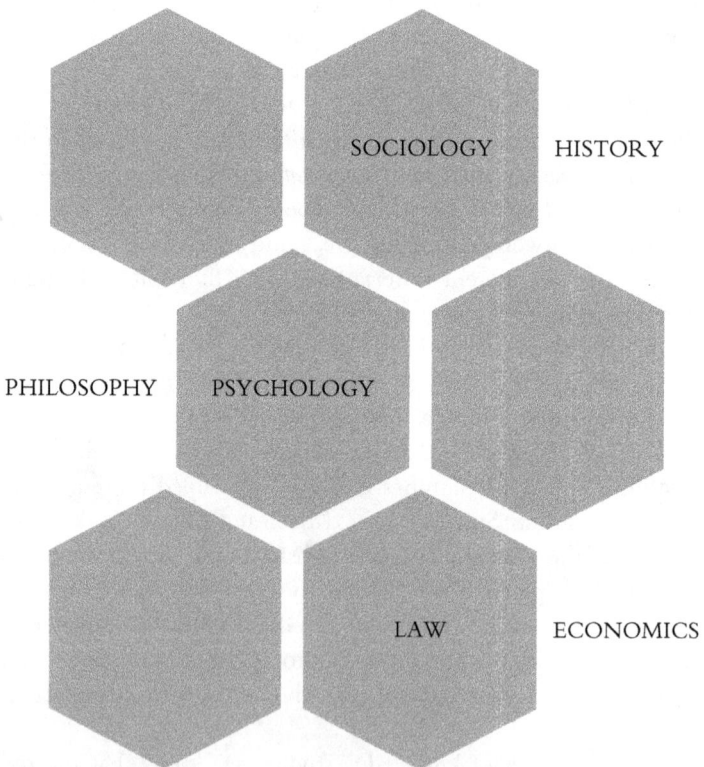

Source: Author

Conclusion

This chapter has shown how IR straddles or embraces the social sciences and the humanities, with the implication that IR is not (only) at home in the social sciences. IR has actually always straddled the social sciences and the humanities, and it will benefit from continuing to embrace both kinds of science. However, rigorous interventions will be necessary to spell out the advantages and limitations of being at home on both sides of the fence – as well as sitting on the fence. In this respect, semantic changes from International Relations to International Studies or Global Studies seem to offer a very fragile solution, but they may also be indicative of the emotions attached to and the rationale of belonging somewhere. It is a fragile platform on which to build a resilient discipline, and solid foundations require thorough deliberations.

As we saw earlier, Elman and Elman (2001) explored the boundaries and bridges between international history and politics. They conclude in a rather pragmatic and yet meaningful and useful fashion: 'If we can overcome our mutual fears of disciplinary meltdown and exploitation, the subfields have a lot to offer each other. The challenge is to chart the boundaries of a middle position that avoids either outright mimicry or rejection, and to build the institutional bridges to support it' (Elman and Elman, 2001: 36). I subscribe to this vision and generalize it to concern future dialogues between IR's branches within the social sciences and the humanities. It is a very ambitious project requiring numerous negotiations, reconsiderations and engagements outside multiple comfort zones. It promises fewer complaints about the fact that cats do not bark and, more importantly, it will situate IR in the position that the discipline deserves. While it is certainly ambitious, it remains feasible, not least because it mirrors how the discipline is actually composed. What remains is merely the recognition of a fact and the reasoning that turns necessity into a deed.

The chapter has explored IR as a global human science and therefore focused on the assets that the social sciences and humanities can offer IR. This focus does not imply that I do not recognize wider perspectives, including inspiration coming from other sciences. Occasionally, scholars trained in the natural and life sciences have transitioned into IR, including for instance the US mathematician Anatol Rapoport. In the past, prominent railway engineers contributed to path-breaking knowledge about the causes of war (Bloch, 1898), and Biology has always been a source of inspiration (Thayer, 2009; see also Thayer and Hudon, 2010). It is thus widely known that neorealism draws on microeconomics but less known that the latter draws on evolutionary biology. The purpose of this part of the conclusion is not to open a new chapter but to raise just two issues. First, to point to a source of inspiration that IR, as one of the human sciences, can perhaps devote more time to, provided the bridge-building intentions of this chapter and other similar initiatives are successful. Second, to ask with Clifford Geertz (1994) why inspiration from the natural and life sciences has been taboo for so long, whereas such inspiration was highly appreciated historically. It is of course true that some of the transfers ended up in scientific orientations and societal and policy practices that are deemed no longer politically warranted, including social Darwinism, racism and eugenics, to mention just a few.

3

What is a Discipline?

Discipline. From the Latin *discere*, to learn.

Introduction

Having examined its subject matter and situated the discipline in the human sciences (i.e. in the combined environment of the social sciences and the humanities), we should address an issue that goes to the bone of this book but which is strangely avoided in much IR disciplinary self-reflection: 'What is a discipline?' The term 'discipline' might appear on every second page of any given IR book but seldom in the index, indicating that it is not handled in a focused or structured fashion. Without a solid conceptualization of 'discipline', whatever is claimed about it will rest on shaky ground or, at worst, be irrelevant. One factor explaining why poor conceptualization is the case may be that examinations of 'the discipline' have focused on the discipline as such and not on the discipline in the context of the changing role and dynamics of scientific disciplines in modern society (for an exception, see Buzan and Little, 2001). A second factor may be the typical reduction of 'discipline' to either its theories or various article metrics. A third factor may be that comparisons between IR and other disciplines are based on impressions about other disciplines, such as the odd idea that political science has a well-defined distinct subject matter and a core of theories and methods about which there is widespread consensus.

It follows that, to understand how the IR discipline has changed over time and how it has changed with the changing context of disciplinary knowledge, there is quite some work to do. It seems to me that we are walking in circles not only in relation to subject matter and social science but also the discipline. This is a different way of saying that debates during the early decades of the 21st century are somewhat similar to debates in the 1950s or the 1980s.

I aim to break the vicious circle by means of three steps. First, I address the key issue of what a scientific discipline is. My reasoning is that, before we can argue about IR's disciplinary status, we need to understand the social processes of discipline formation. Not many scholars can help us but the sociologist Rudolf Stichweh offers some very interesting ideas about the process of discipline formation and reproduction, so he is the obvious choice to guide us (Stichweh, 1992; 2003). Second, by drawing on general discipline characteristics, I outline how the IR discipline evolved over time and how it compares to potential alternatives. Finally, given that a fair share of debates on disciplinarity versus interdisciplinarity hinge on normative preferences, I assess the most important budget lines, that is, look into the benefits *and* the costly ramifications of arguing that IR is not a discipline. With the costs out in the open, the stakes in the ongoing debates become clear and can therefore inform future debates.

What is a discipline?

While scientific disciplines tend to be sticky, they do not transcend time and space; they emerge somewhere and at some time. Moreover, they are not etched in stone but dynamic entities and, once created, scholarly communities tend to adapt disciplines to changing circumstances. Disciplines are social and institutional facts and therefore relatively stable, albeit open to contestation and change.[1] They are vitally and literally dependent on reproduction by means of multiple micro-practices. If they are reproduced, disciplines live. If they are not reproduced, they perish. Hence it is possible to study both the history and the sociology of scientific disciplines (Stichweh, 1992; 2001).

To better understand the nature of scientific disciplines, we can greatly benefit from drawing on the insights of an expert on disciplines, Rudolf Stichweh (2001). There are three reasons why Stichweh is an excellent guide. He provides a comprehensive analysis of scientific disciplines in general. Moreover, he seems not to have been primed by IR self-reflection, so his external view (i.e. external to IR) can help break our intellectual path-dependencies. Finally, he enables the inclusion of subdisciplines, a term that is rarely applied to the undergrowth of the discipline.

Stichweh (2001) points out that disciplines assumed their key function as late as the 19th century:

> Only the nineteenth century established real disciplinary communication systems. Since then the discipline has functioned as a unit of structure formation in the social system of science, in systems of higher education, as a subject domain for teaching and learning in schools, and finally as the designation of occupational and professional roles. Although the processes of differentiation in science are going on all the time, the scientific discipline as a basic unit of structure formation is stabilized by these plural roles in different functional contexts in modern society. (p. 13727)

Stichweh (1992) also points out that many studies of the development of scientific disciplines 'assume an environment of differentiated disciplines and attempt to explain how and why a new discipline ... emerges' (p. 4).[2] It is important to understand that he is aiming at something entirely different from these 'many studies', namely understanding the macro-historical 'preconditions for the establishment of scientific disciplines per se' (Stichweh, 1992: 4). This aim takes him back to the 18th and 19th centuries, to contending ways of defining disciplines and to the development of systems of communication, scientific communities, professions, the nexus between specialized publications and scientific research, and the idea of research-based higher education.

Stichweh is very confident, perhaps surprisingly confident, regarding the future of scientific disciplines. He views subdisciplinary differentiation as a process without any impact on 'the drivers of internal differentiation in modern science'. Moreover, he argues that interdisciplinarity and transdisciplinarity 'do not at all conflict with the disciplinary structure of modern science' (Stichweh, 2003: 88; see also Stichweh, 1992: 13-14).

This observation points to a second feature of IR disciplinary reflection: the almost complete lack of interest in research on the formation of subdisciplines. Finally, Stichweh takes the emergence of the knowledge society as an indication of the continued relevance of disciplinary knowledge, both within scientific institutions and across modern societies.

Stichweh's comprehensive approach to the study of scientific disciplines implies that disciplinary studies must consider the entire disciplinary infrastructure, consisting of conventions, associations, specialized journals, a body of research literature, specialized discourses, textbooks, readers, book series, funding agencies and mythologies of origin – for the making of disciplines includes a degree of myth formation. Within anthropological research, myths play an important role and are thus relevant for the study of the life forms of those who happen to populate the IR community, which is characterized by its own set of professional norms, rules, ceremonies, rituals and prizes (see Chapter 6). In this context, John Kane (2008) makes an important argument for how

> the myth, being mythical, never accurately described American realities, for the function of myth is not to reflect and report the superficial realities of this or any other moment. The domain of myth is not empirical reality but imagination, and the source of its sustenance is not reason but faith. One of the functions of myth is to provide people with a deeper story, a narrative that can encompass their own individual stories and give them meaning, worth, and hope, connected by something more than mere contingency. (p. 5)[3]

It seems to me that there are several connections with how newcomers to a discipline undergo various rituals and are gradually socialized, for instance by means of PhD programmes, into prevalent norms and myths about the history of their discipline. The nature of myths also explains why it takes more than a few items of counter-evidence to rebuff the myth of the 1919 foundation (see Leira and de Carvalho, 2018).

The making of the IR discipline

What applies to the nature of scientific disciplines in general also applies to IR. In historical terms, IR was a latecomer. Stichweh's (1992) observation that many studies of the development of scientific disciplines take for granted a pre-existing environment into which the new discipline is born is especially valid for IR. The fathers and mothers of IR created the new discipline in an environment populated by disciplines such as Law, Sociology, History, Philosophy and Economics. In this context, Stichweh (1992) points out an important feature of inventions: 'Like most inventions, disciplines are not the result of a lucky moment, a singular event, a founding impulse, or an institutional innovation. They represent the cumulative and unforeseeable result of a large number of innovations and changes' (p. 4). Dan Little (2019) concurs:

> But we now understand that the creation of a field of science is a social process with a great deal of contingency and path-dependence. The institutions through which science proceeds – journals, funding agencies, academic departments, Ph.D. programs – are all influenced by the particular interests and goals of a variety of actors, with the result that a field of science develops (or fails to develop) with a huge amount of contingency.

These observations are key to understanding the futility of the pro- and con-1919 controversy. On the one hand, pro-1919 representatives refer to the social environment of the Versailles peace treaty negotiations. Ernst-Otto Czempiel (1965), for instance, prominently highlights a significant meeting at the Hôtel Majestic in Paris and argues that IR was born on 30 May 1919 (p. 272). On the other hand, the con-1919 camp (e.g. de Carvalho et al, 2011) point to a book published in 1900 in New York and the political science department at Columbia University, which began teaching IR in 1880, as indicators of 1919 being a myth. They seem to subscribe to Vitalis' claim that the discipline 'was founded on a racist "white supremacist" outlook' (de Carvalho et al, 2011: 749). In short, both camps point to single events as being of significance for the genesis of a scientific discipline. The alternative is to recognize the cumulative effect of many beginnings, including lessons learned about the beginnings that eventually did not make it.[4] In any case, as mentioned earlier, what matters is not the origins but the repetitions of practices.

The modest beginnings of International Relations can be traced back to the early 20th century, when the first academic chairs were established, the first specialized journals appeared, an important League of Nations committee began to outline the study of international relations, and several professors outlined templates for an International Relations discipline. Yet IR did not truly come of age until the 1950s or 1960s. Obviously, it is rather simple to describe the development in Whiggish terms, and many have done so. However, the topic appears ideal for Foucault's genealogical method. There were many beginnings, and progress was not always linear. In addition to progress, there have also been closures and coincidences have played a role. Hedley Bull (1972) is one of the few to warn against Whiggish narratives, emphasizing that the first responsibility of every new generation is not to make advances but to avoid the discipline sliding backwards.

Trajectories and junctions

As we have seen, it became increasingly popular during the 19th century to organize knowledge into scientific disciplines, and disciplinary historiography points to a remarkable proliferation of disciplines.[5] The IR discipline is one of the outcomes of this, at the time, relatively novel way of organizing scientific knowledge. While disciplines are often presented as coherent sites for the production and communication of knowledge, they have many different origins, birthplaces and components. The IR discipline is no exception. Given the multiple origins, birthplaces and components, analysts doing research on the history of the discipline have ample opportunity to cherry-pick their favourite dimension(s) and to compose (meta-)narratives about disciplinary identity, purpose and history on this basis.

While the early *discipline* of IR was a product of interwar aspirations to win the peace, the *field* of international relations has a considerably longer history and provides important items of disciplinary scaffolding. During the late 19th century, transnational networks of public intellectuals and leaders of social movements were widespread, which functioned to some extent within institutionalized settings, such as the International Peace Bureau in Berne, the Inter-Parliamentary Union and the Union of International Associations. In this context, the two peace conferences in 1898 and 1907 in The Hague were major events. This was the constraining and enabling context within which IR disciplinary activities could develop. However, the discipline first had to be imagined and subsequently launched before any talk of disciplinary trajectories.

Disciplines bring together a broad range of components, including funding streams, specialized journals and book series, theories and methodologies, professional associations, university institutions (departments, chairs, professorships, teaching programmes) and conferences. Approaches focusing on disciplinary communication by means of journals are increasingly popular and occasionally produce great insights. For good reason, however, they are obviously limited to just one part of the disciplinary infrastructure, and analysts should therefore resist the temptation to draw general conclusions about the discipline. Thinking theoretically about international or global affairs has a long pedigree and overlaps with (yet is also significantly different from) the history of the discipline. Disciplined theoretical thinking is also different from the intellectual history of thinking more broadly about 'the international'. The focus in this section is on the discipline, although the overlaps between the three dimensions – disciplinary components, thinking the international and intellectual history – are significant, and we should be able to acknowledge both their distinctive pedigrees and overlaps.

The increasing number of institutions and departments devoted to the study of international affairs not only provided institutional frameworks for analysts and scholars, but they also enabled the exchange of ideas (guest lectures, short-term visits and so forth, i.e. the entire infrastructure we now tend to take for granted). Moreover, the number of journals significantly facilitated transnational communication. Annual pan-European meetings – the summer school in Geneva and ISC meetings – strengthened transnational networks and a growing sense of belonging to a European scholarly community.

While the IR discipline has many birthplaces around the world, Europe was one of its key centres until the Second World War. The density of the discipline's components was sufficient to constitute a critical mass and essentially kick off the new discipline. Academic chairs, departments and specialized institutes were created, and the first specialized journals were launched. During its short period of active existence (1928–39), the ISC gathered many of the scholars who realized a need for the discipline or the study of international relations more broadly. In this fashion, the ISC promoted opportunities for networking and community building (i.e. some of the key functions of professional associations). The ISC membership reflected the membership of the League of Nations and was thus predominantly European, all meetings being held in Europe. In addition to the ISC, it is telling how almost all of the Nobel Peace Prizes were given to Europeans (of a liberal orientation) during the early decades of the 20th century. Finally, as Ann Tickner (1999) points out, the discipline was founded by male scholars (p. 9).

Public intellectuals in the European peace movement (e.g. Bertha von Suttner) and the working-class movement (e.g. Rosa Luxemburg) did engage in thinking about international and/or global affairs, but they were typically situated outside the confines of the emerging academic discipline. The IR discipline (and its representatives) emerged without exception within the imperial centres of the world: in Europe, the US, Japan and the Ottoman empire. The key issue of the emerging discipline was not only war and peace but the equally controversial issues of empire, race and faith. Being part of the wider intellectual and political-ideological currents at the time, many IR scholars promoted racism, their empire and western civilization (Hobson, 2012). These issues were also addressed by influential thinkers and politicians outside academia but within the empires, such as Zhou Enlai (based on years of living in Paris), Sayyid Qutb (based on his US travels) and Mahatma Gandhi (based on living in South Africa and India, which were part of the British empire).

If conceptualizing international affairs was the main purpose of the liberal thinkers at the time, they also engaged in meta-reflections about their endeavour. Part of the liberal project was to educate and promote research-based rational policies. While the former prompted examinations of the international mind and the processes through which it could be achieved, the latter concerned the aspiration to build a 'new science'. They called it different things: 'a field of study', 'the study of international relations', 'the international branch of politics' and 'a discipline'. No matter the labels, liberal thinkers strongly believed they had to be 'scientific'.[6] During the two interwar decades, the discipline actually grew, and they were driving the process, providing most of the infrastructure required by a discipline, including new chairs, institutes, international cooperation and journals. They engaged in an abundance of activities. It is not difficult to understand that all the action prompted a considerable optimism, pushing the pessimism of the intellect aside.

First, a discipline does not simply pop up and then begin its existence; instead, it emerges and evolves, and at some point it becomes meaningful to explore the growth of a discipline that has been constituted over time. In the early years, those devoting their time and research to international issues, who shared an interest in defining the scientific study of international relations (i.e. an interest in addition to addressing and being concerned about contemporary world politics) included historians, lawyers, sociologists, philosophers and the like. Second, a discipline may become more mature but it does not reach a terminus, an end state. A discipline frozen in time is at best at severe risk of becoming irrelevant and at worst a collection of orthodox world-views.

Some developments are shaped by individuals such as Quincy Wright, who did not reject the idea of IR as an autonomous discipline. He agreed with those who argued that IR has a much wider subject matter than political science, as it covers not only politics but also strategic, economic and social affairs (Meynaud, 1953: 109). Unfortunately for the development of IR, however, Wright's successor as president of the International Political Science Association (IPSA), William A. Robson, was of the view that International Relations was an 'indivisible part' of Political Science.

The building blocks of a discipline include institutional structures, sustained discursive structures, scholarly identities, ideas about and processes of professionalization. These are all process variables, social/institutional facts that are in need of reproduction for the discipline stay alive and that depend on micro-practices to be sustainable. In terms of the continuity of processes, the ISC infrastructure included annual meetings as well as national committees on international studies. After the ISC was discontinued, the British national committee nonetheless carried on. Among other activities, it organized the Bailey conferences which, after the British International Studies Association (ISA) was launched, eventually turned into the annual BISA conference, which remained the biggest annual conference in the field in Europe for 40 years (Buzan, 2019).

After the Second World War, the discipline's centre of gravity shifted to the US. The combination of emigré scholars (Rösch 2014), generous funding, an increasingly solid institutional infrastructure and, as a consequence of the emerging Cold War, an urgent need to know the world gave rise to a unique conjuncture and a configuration of components. In the US, the discipline became a blend of positivism, a distinctly conceived social science, within which the emerging political science departments simply subsumed the study of international politics.[7] While the Cold War produced a need for knowledge, it also prompted a strong anti-communist ideological atmosphere, which in turn produced a distinct theoretical form: specifically, the behavioural conception of social science. In a divided Europe, the emigré scholars were missing, funding was limited and the institutional infrastructure was weak and predominantly conservative. Focused on reconstructing the continent and facing the challenges of decolonization, Europe felt the need for knowledge about the world less urgently than the US. In the new independent states of what was starting to be referred to as the 'Third World', resources were even more limited than in Europe, which probably explains why some of the UN economic commissions became the institutional framework for theorizing, for instance producing *dependencia* theory.

Since the mid-1990s, the discipline has developed more evenly. Funding streams are no longer only or mainly North American or European. While they are still highly uneven in their authorship and readership, specialized journals, textbooks and book series increasingly reflect a global community. Some studies are increasingly critical of centric conceptions, not least Eurocentrism (Hobson, 2012), whereas Sinocentrism and other centric perspectives are growing. Scholars in the new emerging centres of IR scholarship are often supportive of centrist perspectives. All major countries and regions have their own professional associations, and, while the ISA conventions increasingly function as a de facto global marketplace for ideas, networks and commerce, the World International Studies Committee (WISC) has become more institutionalized and is extending its activities.[8] The combined output of professional associations in terms of conferences has become truly impressive if not overwhelming. While ever more universities boast of IR departments, chairs, professorships and teaching programmes, the interdisciplinary vogue among university management and 'science bureaucracies' might succeed in undermining the core of disciplinary knowledge.

Root causes of disciplinary growth

In this section, I shall explore the growth of IR by means of two different models. In the first model, historians of the discipline of IR and meta-studies analysts more generally draw a useful distinction between external and internal factors to explain the evolution of the discipline (Schmidt, 1998; Friedrichs, 2004; Holden, 2006, Valbjørn, 2008). External factors include, for instance, shifting configurations of polarity in the international system. Two examples suffice for illustrative purposes. The first, the so-called Twenty Years' Crisis (1919-39), was characterized by the failure of the League of Nations, by liberal internationalism more generally and by the general turbulence of the otherwise long-standing multipolar international order. The two first features especially provoked fierce criticism and gradually empowered realist positions and propositions (Carr, 1939/1946; Morgenthau, 1946; Wight, 1946; Fox, 1949). In this fashion, the dynamics of world politics triggered changes in the balance of power among academic conceptions of the nature of the emerging discipline.

The second example is the significant impact of the Cold War on the discipline and the theories that provide the discipline with a sense of identity. Specifically, the usefulness for state and society of various area studies was determined to some degree by east–west dynamics: centres for 'communist studies' proliferated in the west, just as specialized centres popped up in the east (e.g. focusing on North America). In this perspective, we should expect the end of the Cold War also to have an impact on how we theorize international relations (see Allan and Goldman, 1992). For the same reason, the redirection of funding from 'eastern' area studies to centres for Middle East Studies is not particularly surprising. In this perspective, Europe seemed destined to become whole and free again and in urgent need of 'European integration studies', without any accompanying additives, whether western or eastern. By contrast, internal factors are associated with the inner dynamics of disciplinary developments.

So-called great debates among academics have winners and losers. The winners are subsequently predominant in representing the discipline, outlining its evolution and defining what counts as progress. The 1940s and 1950s are often said to be characterized by a great debate between idealism and realism – and the realists won. At the very least, this applies to the trajectories in one of the heartlands of the discipline during the Cold War: the US. The discipline consequently evolved, and it is hardly surprising that the realist tradition has been seen as predominant in North America. In Europe, however, developments were significantly different (Jørgensen, 2000; Jørgensen and Ergul Jorgensen, 2020), which might suggest that we should expect a degree of regional variation. Second, early debates in American political science spilled over to inform the trajectories of IR in the US, demonstrating the power of internal scientific determinants (Schmidt, 1998). Third, according to the internal factor model, the development of IR has been marked by changing patterns of sources of inspiration. At times and in some places, developments within economics have served as such sources, explaining the import of templates created within Economics (e.g. rational choice, game theory, principal agent models). At other times and in other places, sociology has been mined for insights and has yielded templates (e.g. constructivism, sociological institutionalism). Finally, given the generalizing aspirations that characterize major parts of Political Science and IR, it is only logical that area studies characterized by empirical sensibility and scepticism towards general models have been stigmatized. This tendency includes European Studies, and scholars have been told by the generalizers to forget about European specifics and instead to apply seemingly universal political science templates, created somewhere and for some purpose but usually not in Europe and not with the objective of understanding processes of European integration. In a wider perspective, it seems that each distinct area study has its own experiences with encounters with the disciplinary generalizers (see e.g. Khalidi, 2003; Mitchell, 2003; Valbjørn, 2004; Stevens et al, 2018). Obviously, some combination of the external and the internal can be imagined. However, such combinations would not alter the fact that the external/internal distinction offers an excellent starting point for research on factors explaining the growth of the discipline.

One starting point does not exclude other points of departure. As an alternative to the internal and external factor models, I suggest the application of what has been referred to as a cultural-institutional approach to disciplinary dynamics (Jørgensen and Knudsen, 2006: 3-6), that is, a perspective emphasizing cultural factors such as the political and academic culture of countries or regions as well as the importance of institutional factors at different levels: department, university, national science bureaucracies and professional associations. More specifically, the approach consists of three explanatory variables: political culture; the organizational culture of science bureaucracies, university systems and professional associations; and the customs and academic discourses within the social sciences and humanities. Clearly, the model provides considerably more room for manoeuvre than the internal/external binary, even if the internal option includes a distinction between internal discipline and internal academia. The political culture of countries and regions appears to be significant; after all, it was primarily the processes of political transition that rendered the introduction of western-style IR possible in east and central Europe. Similarly, it was the 1993 promise of future accession to the EU that created a massive demand for knowledge about European integration and governance in the region.

The IR discipline and its subdisciplines

The archetypical image of the relationship between IR and the subdiscipline category is to regard IR itself as a subdiscipline of some bigger and more established discipline (e.g. Law, Political Science). The objective of this section is to make a U-turn to explore IR and its subdisciplines. The simple reason for doing so is that IR seems to be a mature discipline featuring an exquisite capacity to generate numerous subdisciplines. Box 3.1 illustrates the rich undergrowth of IR subdisciplines. It is somewhat strange that the proliferation of subdisciplines has not attracted more attention. However, there are exceptions. Thus, the Central European University's IR department acknowledges 'the two major sub-disciplines of security studies and international political economy'.[9] Indeed, security studies is often listed as a subdiscipline. The existence of multiple subdisciplines sometimes prompts doubts among scholars about IR as an academic discipline (Puchala, 2003: 9). My argument takes the opposite view. The emergence of subdisciplines suggests that the discipline is thriving and that the contents of Box 3.1 should not be deplored but celebrated.

Obviously, the outlined perspective on IR and its subdisciplines will be of limited interest to those who do not recognize the discipline. It will just increase their uneasiness. However, for those

---

Box 3.1: An overview of IR subdisciplines

International organization
Global governance
Security studies
Integration studies
International political economy
Peace studies
International gender studies
International civil society organizations studies, including social
  movements
Studies of transnational companies
International institutions
Diplomacy
War studies
Regional studies
Foreign policy studies (including foreign policy analysis)
International political theory
European studies (to a limited degree)
Intelligence and espionage studies

---

who do recognize the discipline and who want to contribute to it, it seems to me that more attention to the subdisciplines of IR and the role they play can potentially relieve some of the pressure on an occasionally overstretched discipline. It is not a totalitarian discipline about everything.

In terms of substantive understandings, approaches employed and critical mass of scholars, the subdisciplines show considerable variation around the world but the strengthening of communication (specialized journals and conferences) and global scholarly networks such as WISC will make the subdisciplines more resilient and viable.

Are there any attractive alternatives to discipline?

Having specified the nature of disciplines, we should ask if there are any viable alternatives. The answer is easy, as there are always alternatives in the human sciences and always more approaches than arrivals, more critique than targets. It is therefore hardly controversial to point out that alternative categories do exist. But are they attractive? Categories for ordering the production of scientific IR knowledge come in different versions. In this section, I outline the three main categories, one of which comes in two different versions.

The first way of categorizing scientific knowledge is to go back to pre-disciplinary historical categories. Klaus-Gerd Giesen (2006) applies three categories (historicism, encyclopedism, positivism) to the production of IR knowledge in a selection of French-speaking countries. While it is a rare choice, Giesen eminently demonstrates the value added of the chosen approach. The primary reason for the usefulness of the categories is that they are applicable across disciplines and they highlight patterns of thinking that would not otherwise appear in such a clear fashion. One analyst of the changing structures of knowledge production suggests that the old and contemporary knowledge forms share features in common:

> In the 17th and 18th centuries 'encyklopedik' was understood as a particular science in its own right dealing with the classification and order of knowledge. At the beginning of the 21st century this role seems to

have been taken over by the ever-expanding discourse on cross-, inter- and transdisciplinarity. Still, it might be that these two historically distant perspectives on the orders of knowledge have more in common than we tend to think. (Jordheim, 2012)

Whether or not the old and new categories share something or have something in common, the old categories would not appear to offer proper alternatives to disciplinary categorization. They enable us to acknowledge how patterns of thinking within IR, for instance historicism, are also practised within other disciplines. Moreover, they enable us to explore how the configuration of the categories varies across time and space, for instance how positivism has informed IR scholarship in some but not other regions.

The second alternative concerns the option of interdisciplinary research, that is, a form of research that time and again has demonstrated its capacity to generate great insights and contribute to research that is directly relevant for modern society (see e.g. Kratochwil, 2018). This book is not about the value of interdisciplinary research but rather about the role of disciplines in general and IR in particular. To understand the different positions, I draw a distinction between interdisciplinary research *with* and *without* disciplines.

According to some, the notion of a paradigm is so broad that it can be used as a synonym for 'discipline', or at least it bears a family resemblance to it. By contrast, 'interdisciplinary studies' cannot be an alternative to 'discipline' simply because the key premise of interdisciplinarity is the existence of disciplines. In other words, interdisciplinarity without discipline is a spineless, non-viable construction that seems to have taken root in the minds of science managers and some scholars. In short, alternatives to discipline do exist, but their attraction is limited and they do not seem to be viable alternatives.

Conceptions of interdisciplinary research with disciplines come in two versions: IR is either in or out. Scholars in favour of IR as an interdisciplinary field of study often prefer 'International Studies' (Aalto et al, 2011). Importantly, Aalto defends disciplinarity, pointing out that without discipline we have messy empirical realities, specialized knowledge and more.

To the degree that disciplines play a role in this conception, which it does not always, IR is seen as the nexus of all sorts of disciplines. Proponents simply do not believe that IR should be one of the disciplines contributing to interdisciplinary research. They tend to highlight how frequently IR scholars borrow from disciplines while adding an international dimension. However, they pay less attention to how frequently all scholars tend to borrow from disciplines that are not their own. It is well known that this can be done in more or less sophisticated fashions, but trans-disciplinary transfers cannot be used as something that disqualifies a given discipline. Moreover, to be a relevant partner in interdisciplinary research, IR must offer good scope, guiding research questions, theory and methodology – the stuff that makes disciplines – otherwise it risks irrelevancy.

The second reason is simply that it takes time and extensive conversation and negotiations to conclude how exactly the changing nature of what we study has an impact on our field of study. Ehsanul Haque (2012) makes some intriguing observations on the 'Permeability of Disciplinary Boundaries in the Age of Globalization':

> In a globalized world, we witness an entirely new, unprecedented form of knowledge production where the creation and utilization of knowledge is no longer seen as a linear process. In fact, the forces of globalization demand multiple disciplines to unravel and scientists transgress/cross disciplinary boundaries in their search for new knowledge creation and dissemination. Against this backdrop, this chapter particularly reflects on the interdisciplinary character of International Relations (IR) – a successful and fascinating interdisciplinary subject having infinite boundaries. While IR is a full-blown, autonomous, and accomplished academic discipline, its hybrid curricula bring complementary strengths and enlarged perspectives from a diverse array of disciplines including Political Science, History, Economics, Sociology, Philosophy, and the like in order to address the ever-increasing complexities and broader issues as well as to impart unified knowledge and produce cognitive advancement. (p. 13)

Haque then proceeds to argue how the interdisciplinary breadth of such IR learning benefits students and practitioners in the field. The study demonstrates how, in the domain of IR, interdisciplinarity supplements disciplinary learning, thereby equipping students to respond to challenges that spill over the discipline boundaries to work at the confluence of multiple disciplines, and to develop research trajectories that do not conform to standard disciplinary approaches. In his view, students develop a 'meta-knowledge' of multiple disciplines, methods and epistemologies, and learn how to reflectively integrate and synthesize different perspectives. Finally, Haque concludes that such interdisciplinarity promotes quality research and contributes to solving new problems that cannot be addressed within the individual disciplines alone.

The third suggested alternative is IR as a hybrid discipline. Felix Grenier (2015) advances this idea by creating a contradiction between discipline and diversity and by making a distinction between fox and hedgehog disciplines. Grenier believes that disciplines restrict diversity and marginalize plurality. The main characteristics of his hedgehog discipline are exclusion, marginalization, policy orientation, a narrow understanding of audiences and limited methodologies. By contrast, the main characteristics of a fox discipline include the capacity to do many things, cherishing diversity, hybridity, pluralism, methodological pluralism, having no fixed borders and radical discontinuity. Grenier believes that plural research communities are not the same as incoherence.

Studies of disciplinary history have mushroomed in the last two decades, leading to a thorough reconsideration of the origins and trajectories of the discipline. That is all good but it begs the question of whether there can be disciplinary history, a veritable cottage industry, without a discipline. I think not. But what are the benefits of growing a discipline? The next section addresses the issue.

Why discipline?

Why is it important to insist on IR as a discipline, possibly situated within the human sciences? In short, it is mainly due to survival as well as power, pride and prestige, features that are important in the field we study (global affairs) but also for our field of study (IR). In this section, I outline four extended answers, beginning with the observation that it's a jungle out there – so beware! Next, I briefly account for a few historical examples of opposition to the disciplinary enterprise before moving on to the frequent examples of sniping at the discipline. Finally, I describe the stakes in and the costs of going with the alternatives to discipline.

That it's a jungle out there is a 100-year-long experience. The academic world is an anarchy in which survival depends on self-help. Predators are ever ready to attack those whom they deem weak. In addition to direct attacks at close range, there are institutional inertia and well-known strategies of neglect, denigration, repressive tolerance, downsizing and marginalization. Many readers of this book will have their own experiences or know of multiple cases. As the editors of the *British Journal of Politics and International Relations* observe about the British case, 'for many decades, "British politics" privileged the "domestic" over the "international"; and "international relations" colluded to create intellectual space for itself' ('Editorial: Studying British Politics', 1999: 7).[10]

As for historical examples, the 100-year experience began on day one. The enthusiastic founders of the new science recognized the rationale for creating a science of international relations and began contemplating how it should be defined, its function within academia and in society, as well as ways of organizing it. Over time, more operational thinking replaced or complemented contemplation and the enthusiastic founders experienced stiff opposition. Historians, economists, sociologists and others within existing disciplines tended to think that what they saw as a field of study would best be studied within existing disciplinary boundaries, that is, within their distinct disciplines. An early example is James Bryce (1922), who in a preface to *International Relations* claimed that 'History is the best – indeed the only – guide to a comprehension of the facts as they stand' (cited in Bull, 1972). Especially during the early days of the discipline, there were very few IR chairs and personal dispositions mattered. Thus, Alfred Zimmern was an important founder of the discipline, but his successor at Oxford, Agnes Hedlam-Morley, was no friend of IR, and thought, like Bryce, that IR was and should remain a subfield of History (Hall, 2012; see also Owens, 2018; 2019; Zimmern, 1939). In the UK, universities in the Oxbridge tradition were characterized by strong institutional inertia, implying that product R&D was left largely to the red brick universities of the 1960s and 1970s. Old traditional universities on the European continent and elsewhere were no different from Oxbridge.

Sniping at IR is a constant. After some time, some of the enthusiastic founders entertained second thoughts. The author of *The Twenty Years' Crisis, 1919–1939: An Introduction to the Study of International Relations*, E.H. Carr (1939/1946), who wrote about the science of international politics, became less enthusiastic, to say the least, a dozen years later: 'I have long thought that International Relations is a rag-bag into which one is entitled to put anything one please. Charles Manning's attempt at the LSE [London School of Economics] to turn it into some sort of organized self-contained subject was a fiasco' (cited in Haslam, 1999: 253).[11] There are numerous other examples from the 1950s. Successive IPSA presidents subscribed to different perspectives on the issue, and rapporteurs responsible for UNESCO reports exchanged fire. One such rapporteur opined that 'the teaching of International Relations within departments of political science is in our opinion the correct solution' (cited in Manning, 1957a: 134), only to be countered by another rapporteur, Manning himself, who passionately argued that IR should be recognized as a distinct discipline. One reviewer in *The Economist* was sceptical of 'the so-called social sciences' and their simulation of the natural sciences. Instead, the reviewer saw History as the one and only discipline, whereas the role of 'the so-called social sciences, including the *soi-disant* science of international relations is to act as ancillaries to historical scholarship' (cited in Manning, 1957a: 128). Once again, with ' "Naughty Animal" – a Discipline Chats Back' (Manning, 1957a), Manning returned the compliments.

Sniping at IR is by no means a pursuit that belonged only to the early days of the discipline. In the mid-1960s, when the journal *Cooperation and Conflict* was launched, Niels Andrén (1965) summarized his situation analysis, 'In most countries concerned academic studies of current international affairs have only recently, and gradually been accepted as necessary or useful and legitimate from a scholarly point of view' (p. 1). Similarly, when the *British Journal of Politics and International Relations* was launched, the first editorial was rather dismissive of IR, prompting Steve Smith to defend the discipline. According to Smith (2000), 'the editors made some provocative remarks about the state of the discipline of international relations (IR) in the United Kingdom' (p. 374). Moreover, the sniping comes not just from scholars in other disciplines but occasionally also from within, as in Barry Buzan's (1997) introduction to a book about key figures in the discipline: 'Seen as a whole, the book is a thought-provoking reflection on the fragmentation of the discipline: its lack of almost any generally shared epistemological, methodological, or ontological premises. We would seem to be not only a "divided discipline", but increasingly one with no discernible centre at all' (p. xiii). Four years later, Richard Little joined Buzan in declaring IR a failed intellectual project while also offering a way forward (Buzan and Little, 2001).

The fourth reason it is important to recognize IR as a discipline is the considerable costs involved in rejecting the discipline. In contrast to many scholars, Helen Turton (2015) is keenly aware of the stakes involved. She highlights how the label 'discipline' connotes expertise, rigour and the production of knowledge, emphasizing how rejection of discipline suggests that the discipline is insufficiently developed, fails to meet certain standards and lacks an intellectual pedigree. Moreover, she shows how internal critique may spill over into external critique, thereby reproducing images of divided, directionless and disputatious activities. Finally, she understands that scholars occasionally use internal critique instrumentally to gatekeep and discipline those who define the discipline more broadly than a traditional core. While Turton is more cost-oriented than most, she tends to reduce the costs to images and perceptions, that is, without spelling out how rejection of discipline might cause IR to lose the competition with other disciplines. Marginalization by, or being subsumed within, other disciplines is a 100-year-long experience and a daily reality for many scholars.

Pemberton (2020) describes in detail how those rejecting IR as a distinct discipline during the early 1950s contributed to the assault on the ISC, the first transnational IR association. Two positions are very familiar to contemporary IR scholars. On the one hand, Zimmern imagined IR as a marketplace where IR scholars find insights produced by scientific disciplines and build knowledge about international relations. In the contemporary world, Zimmern's successors have demonstrated their preference for IR as an interdisciplinary field of study, where it is possible to draw freely on all relevant disciplines. For the IR as an interdisciplinary field of study position, diversity is built into the definition and thereby almost guaranteed. Instead of a firm disciplinary hand, analysts prefer a completely free hand. Such a field is consuming and integrating knowledge, but one should not expect the field of study to be a source of inspiration for scholars within other disciplines. According to Buzan and Little (2001) one of the consequences is that IR has failed as an intellectual project, the symptom being that people working in other disciplines generally do not find much inspiration in it. We import but do not export. The interdisciplinary field of study position sees little need for discipline in the sense of cultivating integrated approaches to the field we study.

At the same time, Manning pleads for IR as a distinct discipline. However, it was a third position that defined IR as a dimension of political science both in the US and at the international level, political science itself being defined as one of the social sciences. Pemberton describes how Morgenthau, by highlighting international politics, aligned himself with the third position. The context of the assault on the ISC thus demonstrates how contending discourses have coexisted and continue to coexist. IR became a marginalized dimension of IPSA and lost the promotion of the League of Nation's successor, UNESCO. The outcome had significant consequences for the discipline, one of the vital ones being that IR essentially lost the 1950s and parts of the 1960s, thus matching the characteristics of Robert Musil's *The Man without Qualities*. The view in several parts of the world was and remains that IR is and should be a branch, a subfield or a field of study within the discipline of political science. That IR and political science follow different trajectories did not matter or was worst for the IR scholars. IR's third and fourth debates have hardly occurred within political science, globalization has hardly been discovered by Comparative Politics, and political theory/thought has only recently discovered the world that exists beyond national boundaries (Armitage, 2004; 2012). The actually existing diversity is tolerated as long as it stays within the confines of political science. IR publications count if they appear in general political science journals, a regulatory convention that makes the *American Political Science Review* the gold standard.

For a discipline that is not recognized in the wider scientific community, that is not promoted and that lacks self-confidence, IR could be said to be without qualities. IR regained some strength only in the late 1960s and, notably in terms of organization, this occurred predominantly at the national level, not the transnational level.[12] This demonstrates how the combination of internal and external factors had devastating consequences for the discipline that *grosso modo* missed growth opportunities during two significant decades of the 20th century.

Conclusion

There are two reasons for this chapter's exploration of what scientific disciplines are. First, we should know the environment into which IR was born and in which the discipline subsequently grew up; second, we need to know the nature of scientific disciplines before we can discuss the way in which IR is a discipline. Moreover, instead of continuing to walk in circles, I propose a path forward so that debates in the 21st century can potentially be different from debates in the 1950s or the 1980s. Drawing on Stichweh's understanding of scientific disciplines, the second section outlined the discipline's trajectories. Generally speaking, the early 20th century was an era of disciplinary beginnings, linked to numerous origins and drawing on a rich repertoire of sources. Most but not all beginnings and origins were in Europe. Nonetheless, as Gareau (1981) points out, a 'shocking but wonderfully ironic aspect of the history of the discipline international relations as typically portrayed in American professional literature is that it is as American as apple pie' (p. 779). Ironic indeed, as the discipline and apple pie both have a past and parallel histories in Europe. It is tempting to claim, on the basis of the available evidence, that the discipline was emerging predominantly in Europe up to the Second World War, and that it was American foundations that directed substantial financial resources to the activities. The third section examined four alternative ways of categorizing scientific knowledge and concluded that, while alternatives exist, they are either flawed or not particularly attractive. The fourth section considered the consequences (intended or unintended) of opting for alternatives. Those in discipline denial tend to adopt a libertarian stance and neglect the high stakes involved in, as well as the costs of, rejecting IR's disciplinary status.

If the Parisian Hôtel Majestic was where the liberal discipline was if not born then at least conceived in 1919, it was in the same buildings that the fate of the discipline's first (quasi-)association, the ISC, was decided a few decades later: first when the German military and the Gestapo occupied the building in 1940 (and stealing the archives), and subsequently as the home of UNESCO, an international organization that has never recognized IR as a discipline.[13]

4

What is Theory?

Introduction

This chapter traces the nature of theory, including changing conceptions of it. Given that the book is about a discipline that is defined to some degree by its theories, such a chapter seems almost obligatory. That scholars often define the discipline by its theories indicates that the significance of theory for the discipline is considerable and, moreover, that exploring the functions of theory for and in the discipline is worthwhile. This chapter is therefore not yet another chapter about the body of IR theories. Nor is it only about *theory* but also about *theorizing*, not least because, as Rosemary Shinko (2006) highlights, 'theorizing is fun' (p. 45) and should be taught. The chapter examines meta-theoretical issues, albeit with a view towards practical rather than hair-splitting *problematiques*.

In the next section I characterize the act of theorizing and outline the functions of theory in a disciplinary context, to avoid some of the potential misunderstandings that might follow from limited specification. The point of departure is to perceive IR as not a static but a dynamic discipline. From such a perspective, it follows that the functions of theory in the discipline change over time, a fact that has not received the attention it deserves. In this context, it is crucial to understand that conceptions of theory also change over time; what counted as theory in the 1930s no longer counts that much in the 1960s or the 2010s. Within IR, the first reference to theory seems to have been made in the 1930s. Subsequently, theory, or rather the meaning of theory for the discipline, has experienced some profound swings and turns, a process that has been strongly marked by geographical variation. For instance, the search for the Holy Grail, in this case a general theory of international politics (TIP), came to an abrupt end around 1970 in some parts of the world (Holsti, 1971) but there was no such search in other parts.

Subsequently, in the third section, I shall demonstrate how the changing conceptions of theory have consequences for the trajectory of the discipline. As we shall see, one function of theory is to provide propositions that can in turn generate questions for empirical research. This connects well with the idea that the discipline should be defined not by its subject matter but by its guiding research questions (see Chapter 1). In this capacity theory contributes to the resilience and autonomy of the discipline, not least because funders of research, who are external to the discipline, are keen to set research agendas and thereby promote their preferred questions. Finally, theory plays a role in the academic power politics within the discipline as well as between disciplines, for instance in status boosting and in IR's legitimacy either as one of the human sciences or as a craft discipline. Scholars making major advances typically make claims about theoretical upgrades (Russell, 1936; Singer, 1960, 1961; Waltz, 1990; Wendt, 1992). In the context of status boosting, theory also plays a role in processes of subdiscipline formation (see Chapter 3), especially in relation to the pronounced and healthy differentiation between general theories (of the discipline) and the more specific theories of the subdisciplines. I conclude the chapter with a plea for a pluralist (yet not boundary-free) concept of theory.

The functions of theory

To avoid becoming embroiled in all sorts of IR theory specifics, let us begin by considering the etymological meanings of the terms 'theory' and 'theorizing'. While 'theory' derives from the Greek word *theōría* (for contemplative abstract thinking) a contrast to *praxis* (doing), 'theorizing' is the praxis of contemplative abstract thinking. In this context, we must take into account how acts of theorizing are given much less attention than their outcome, theory. We need to look briefly into what theorists do when they theorize.[1] According to Donald Puchala (2003), 'The theorists are first and foremost conceptualizers, symbolizers, synthesizers and abstract organizers

... what they have been doing as theorists is painting for us in their writings bold-stroked, broad-brushed pictures of social reality and telling us that the real world is their pictures' (p. 24).[2] To the best of my knowledge this is probably the most concise definition of the theorizing process, so this chapter will explore the functions of the 'bold-stroked, broad-brushed pictures of social reality'; thus it will not have a conventional focus. In most cases, articles and books are about the characteristics of one or more theories (e.g. their qualities in terms of scope, consistency or logics), or their relevance for empirical studies (their applicability), or the purposes a theory might have (for someone). The focus of this chapter is different. It is about the function theories have in processes of discipline formation.

The first step is to acknowledge that theory has multiple functions for scientific disciplines. For the discipline of international relations, theory has a demarcating function vis-à-vis neighbouring disciplines, some of which are reproduced by scholarly communities that may occasionally have hostile attitudes towards IR. Hedley Bull (1972: 30-1) provides one example of the argument, pointing out that theory helps reject the view that the subject can or should be studied in historical terms alone. Bull emphasizes how he, in contrast to hardcore social scientists, cherishes historical dimensions and finds them very valuable, but IR is nevertheless not a branch of History. The second function is that theory makes assumptions explicit, thereby subjecting them to debate (Bull, 1972: 32), a function that Hoffmann and Keohane (1991) also point out. The importance of this function of theory cannot be emphasized too much, especially because it touches one of the demarcation lines between theory and ideology: the former is up for debate and contestation, while the latter belongs to the realm of faith or is untouchable.

Morgenthau (1970) has a very humble approach to the functions of theory. First of all, he emphasizes time and again the limits of theorizing, among other things, with reference to the subject matter of international relations:

> It is only within these limits that theoretical thinking on international relations is theoretically and practically fruitful. Within these limits, a theory of international relations performs the functions any theory performs, that is, to bring order and meaning into a mass of

unconnected material and to increase knowledge through the logical development of certain propositions empirically established. (Morgenthau, 1970: 257)

However, he highlights further functions, drawing an important distinction between intellectual and political functions of theory. In a brilliant response to Martin Wight's (1960) article 'Why is There No International Theory?', Morgenthau (1970) examines the intellectual and political (or practical) functions of theory, arguing that the ramifications of the distinction are significant: 'While this theoretical function of a theory of international relations is no different from the function any social theory performs, its practical function is peculiar to itself' (p. 256).

In this fashion Morgenthau proposes a solution to the distinction and apparent dilemma between the universal and the particular. Whereas the intellectual function is universal, the political–practical functions of theory are particular. According to Morgenthau (1970), drawing on Karl Mannheim's sociology of knowledge, the practical functions of a theory of international relations are *Standortgebunden*, that is, the function 'depends very much upon the political environment within which the theory operates' (p. 257). Morgenthau has limited respect for abstract theorizing and targets behavioural theories as a kind of theory that is nothing but bland abstraction. Instead, he praises theories that are built to understand practical problems, and in this context he outlines four practical functions that theory provides:

- a theoretical justification for political action;
- a critical function, providing a coherent system of thought that embodies sound principles of foreign policy;
- the function of an intellectual conscience, reminding policy-makers about the sound principles they represent but might have forgotten;
- the function of preparing the ground for a new international order that is radically different from the one that preceded it.

Morgenthau adds one more function, the *shielding* function, which protects the academic community from contact with the living political world, 'theorizing for theorizing's sake, an innocuous pastime in which academics engage for the benefit of other academics, without effect upon political reality and unaffected by it' (Morgenthau, 1970: 261). Segments within the contemporary IR community seem eager to throw this characterization at other segments, notably without considering it a relevant self-image.

As demonstrated by the Morgenthau case, the functions of theory represent a contested issue. However, there are several more dimensions to the functions of theory. Max Horkheimer (1937) introduced two such functions, specifically with his distinction between traditional and critical theory. In his perspective, traditional theories have a conservative leaning, accepting things as they are or taking things for granted. By contrast, critical theories have a progressive leaning, problematizing on the basis of an emancipatory telos in existing social relations. In the decades that followed, critical theory developed an intellectual path dependency characterized by its own distinct inertia towards becoming virtually a truth claim. Many scholars take a shortcut, however, referring instead to Robert Cox's (1981) distinction between critical theory and problem-solving theory. No matter the swings and turns of the argument, studies end up criticizing a given targeted theory for legitimizing something that the critic does not like. Especially for poststructuralists, critique is the *raison d'être* for their activities – for which reason the target can be anything.

One additional function can be called *theories as question generators*. As active systems of knowledge production, disciplines are bound to attract attention from other sociopolitical systems, including political, administrative and religious systems. The IR discipline is no exception. There is no lack of actors external to the discipline who want to shape the IR community's research agenda. Whether private foundations, states or advocacy groups, they all have questions and research agendas they want to prioritize. The family of David Davies had a motive when they donated £20,000 to the study of international relations, specifically to create the first university chair in International Relations at what is now Aberystwyth University. In the early years the US foundations – Rockefeller, Carnegie and Ford – played a highly influential role in promoting the study of international relations, during both the interwar years and the Cold War, not only in the US but also in

Europe (Rietzler, 2009; Guilhot, 2011; Kuru, 2017; Morie, 2019; on the Ford Foundation, see Berghahn, 2001). The EU's research programmes play an important role in creating a transnational research community in Europe, but it is a community with a set research agenda.

Given that one of the functions of theories is to ask questions, and thus not to provide answers, IR theorists compete with actors who are external to the discipline, which provides a certain degree of resilience. In other words, theorists contribute to give disciplines a certain degree of autonomy vis-à-vis other systems. Like Morgenthau's critique of the Eisenhower administration, Mearsheimer and Walt's (2003) critique of the Iraq War, which did not make them popular with the Bush administration, was informed by theory. In this context, the type of theory – explanatory, interpretive or normative – does not matter, although the questions generated by the different types of theory show significant variation. Whereas a causal theory such as the (policy) domino theory, which motivated and subsequently legitimized US engagement in the Vietnam War and beyond, might trigger questions about the causal logic of policies, normative theory might prompt a focus on flaws in policy-makers' ethical and normative reasoning. In both cases, theory triggers critical investigations.

The final but not least important function of theory is the reproductive function. A discipline is partly constituted by its theories (and methods), and the processes of constitution are passed on from generation to generation. In the words of Rudolf Stichweh (2001), 'Besides professionalization there is then the effect that the discipline educates its own future research practitioners in terms of the methods and theories constitutive of the discipline' (p. 13729). It follows that if a discipline does not educate its own future practitioners it is looking at future decay.

Changing conceptions of theory

Conceptions of theory vary across time and space. This section outlines the main changes and focuses on five distinct phases (see Table 4.1). It is thus structured by the temporal but includes geo-epistemological variation.

Table 4.1: Changing conceptions of theory

Phase	Period	Key dimensions
1	1919–1940	Ideas, reflections, thought
2	1940–1970	More of the same but also a turn to a more restricted understanding of theory, which was, not least, seen as a source of legitimacy
3	1970–1990	Reproduction of former understandings but also an increased recognition of theorizing as a pluralist undertaking
4	1990–2013	Towards a complete palette of ontological and epistemological orientations
5	2013 to present	Reproductive practices but also distortion and decay of theorizing culture

Phase 1: 1919–1940

During the first four decades of the 20th century, the concept of theory played a remarkably limited role in scholarly reflections on global affairs. Theorizing and applying theory was simply not on the agenda and not at all trendy. In the prominent publications of the early 20th century, the term was generally neither included nor employed. The first to use the term seems to have been Harold Laski (1932), with his theory of international society, followed by Hans Morgenthau (1934) and his theory of disputes. The first comprehensive book on the topic was Frank M. Russell's (1936) *Theories of International Relations*. These three examples are exceptions to the rule, however, and Russell emphasizes this state of affairs by calling the field a terra incognita. Moreover, the meaning of theory was very different from later conceptions. Neither Laski nor Morgenthau explicate what theory means to them or why they employ the term. To Russell (1936), theory simply means, in the characteristic language of the time, 'man's ideas concerning the relationship of independent communities' (p. vi). With this objective in mind, Russell traces the more significant ideas concerning international relations from the earliest time. Apart from a few significant exceptions, interest in theory was thus very limited, and it is no wonder that the function of theory in constituting the discipline was almost non-existent. It should be added that the term 'theory' has a relative, 'thought', and the difference between Russell's understanding of 'theory' and Florence Stawell's (1929) understanding of the term 'thought' seems to be insignificant. Both Russell and Stawell offer retrospectives.

Why is the limited role of theory remarkable? The restraint in employing the term and in explicit theorizing is not at all self-evident. After all, the term 'theory' was widely used in other human sciences, as reflected in the standards of social science at the time (Weber, 1904/1949), Keynes's 'The general theory of employment' (1937), Eduard Meyer's (1902) *Zur Theorie und Methodik der Geschichte*, as well as Max Horkheimer (1937) and his famous distinction between traditional and critical theory. It does not seem far-fetched to conclude that, whereas frequent attempts were made to define the study of international relations, scholars showed less interest in theorizing international relations.

To understand both the absence and later subsequent surges in theory building, it is revealing to look into explanations of the lack of theory in early IR. While E.H. Carr (1939/1946) showed a serious interest in the beginnings of a science, he did highlight that 'the science of international relations is in its infancy' (p. 1). In other words, why expect an infant discipline to be sophisticated in theoretical matters? Morgenthau's explanation focuses, as we saw, on the functions of theory. He essentially argues that the prominent scholars of the interwar years were incapable of theorizing, and claims that realists alone can think theoretically. Hedley Bull (1972) continues the lines of argument started by Carr and Morgenthau, suggesting that, first, the study of IR first had to be defined (Bull's forms of discipline) and, second, political advocacy was a priority:

> The idealists were theorists in the sense that they sought not only to present the history and recent development of international relations, but also to raise general questions as to what they were, how they operated, and how they might be influenced so as to better achieve the objectives of peace and order. But their answers to these questions now strike us as superficial. The 'idealists' were not remarkable for their intellectual depth or powers of explanation, only for their intense commitment to a particular vision of what should happen. (Bull, 1972: 35)

In this fashion, Bull suggests that there is a trade-off between advocacy and theorizing, a trade-off that might also be relevant for contemporary IR.

In terms of variation across space, it is first of all significant that the worldwide distribution of universities was very uneven. Major parts of the world were without universities, so why would anyone expect contributions from these regions to the discipline, including theoretical reflections? For instance, studies of the growth of universities in Africa highlight how 'colonial rule left behind very few universities, the majority of countries did not even have a single university' (Zeleza, 2006).

Phase 2: 1940–1970

This brings us to the second phase and the observation that it is during this phase that theoretical work took off. In the words of Bull (1972), 'The term "theory of international relations" became fashionable only in the mid-1950s, and then only in the United States' (p. 33). This is a very significant double delimitation, including both time and space. It leaves us with a paradox. On the one hand, we have Russell's book, over 500 pages on theories of international relations and, on the other, we have the claim that IR theory was launched only during the 1950s and only in one country. The paradox disappears if we consider how Russell and Bull understand theory differently, that they examine different timelines and that they focus on different spaces. We have seen how Russell understands theory as ideas, whereas Bull (1972) explains how 'By the theory of international politics we may understand the body of general propositions that may be advanced about political relations between states, or more generally about world politics' (p. 30). Moreover, whereas Russell has a global outlook, Bull focuses on developments in English-speaking countries and neglects other countries.

In many ways, the 1950s functioned as an exciting 'experimentarium' for the development of an understanding of what theoretical thinking might entail and, in turn, a capacity to think theoretically. The debates demonstrate why it makes sense to differentiate between different phases, and show how contending visions encounter each other.

The end of the ISC meant an end to a communication system that could have been instrumental for theoretical innovation. However, ISC's international or transnational communication system was replaced by IPSA, which treated IR as a minor subdiscipline at best, hampering theoretical advances at the transnational level. This task was thus left to national venues. National communication systems replaced the ISC, such as the Bailey conferences in the UK, the creation of associations in Japan, South Korea and the US in the late 1950s.[3] In this context, it is relevant to draw attention to the 1954 conference sponsored by the Rockefeller Foundation (Guilhot, 2011). The conference had a double aim: to advance IR as an autonomous discipline and to promote realism as the discipline's theoretical edifice. According to Guilhot's own chapter in his edited volume, the conference was a realist gambit, an opening move. The gambit was not lost on Priscilla Roberts, who emphasizes that the convened scholars, mainly realists of different sorts, were asked to 'consider the emergence in the United States after World War II not simply of the field of International Relations but of the Realist approach to such studies' (Roberts, 2012). David McCourt arrives at the same conclusion, that the conference aimed at equipping the discipline with a realist cornerstone (McCourt, 2020a: 560; 2020b: 11). However, aspirations are not always achieved, and Guilhot concludes that 'The realist gambit, ultimately, was a losing one' (cited from the previously published article, Guilhot, 2008: 301). Nonetheless, according to numerous textbooks, which endlessly present realism as the dominant IR theory, realism was highly successful. According to Bull (1972), however, it was the heyday of a failed attempt to present practical knowledge of a realist orientation as theory: 'not even the best of realist writings can be said to have achieved a high standard of theoretical refinement: they were powerful polemical essays ... but the theory they employed was "soft", not "hard"' (p. 39).

Soon thereafter, Martin Wight compares political theory to international theory and ponders why there is no international theory. By means of the comparison to political theory, Wight shows himself to be as far from behavioural social science as one can get. The same applies to Manning's (1962b) theory of international society and Aron's work from the 1960s, especially his book *Peace and War* and an essay, 'What is a Theory of International Relations?'

(Aron, 1962/1966; 1967). Morgenthau (1962) is clearly a member of the same club. In short, the behavioural revolution triggered a deep split in the IR community, a split that goes to the bone of what theory is and, in turn, a conflict about the identity of the IR discipline, including its boundaries. In addition to these general fault-lines within the discipline, several subdisciplines began to crystallize, for instance foreign policy studies and peace research (Dunn 2005; Carlsnaes 2015).

By the late 1960s, scholars began increasingly to acknowledge that the search for a general theory of international politics had failed (Aron, 1967; Holsti, 1971; 1985; Bull, 1972; Hoffmann, 1977). The intended outcome, to be achieved by means of empiricist induction procedures and an all-inclusive abandonment of political philosophy, failed to materialize, and different scholars offered various explanations of this dead end. They focused less on the unintended consequences, for instance that theorists could escape the conceptual prisons of the term 'theory'. Moreover, they did not recognize that the damage done to the discipline was limited largely to North America, that is, to the region where the general theory endeavour had been strongest. As Herbert Butterfield and Martin Wight drily point out, " 'The theory of international politics' is a phrase without wide currency or clear meaning in this country" (1966: 11). In short, the platform for building an IR within the human sciences had been cleared. It was again open for potential advances.

In terms of variation across space, it is important to remember that major parts of the world had universities but limited academic freedom. Conditions at universities in the Soviet Union, eastern Europe and China did not exactly encourage scholars to engage in theoretical reflection (see e.g. Tyulin, 1997). Moreover, the significant growth of universities in the 'Third World' took off only with decolonization and independence, and the second phase consisted of years of launching programmes of higher education (Woldegiorgis and Doevenspeck, 2013). Referring to these new programmes, Paul Zeleza (2006) points out how 'there was the need to make them more relevant to Africa's developmental needs and socio-cultural contexts and more accessible to students of different social backgrounds'. This helps us to understand some of the theoretical departures that characterize the next phase.

Phase 3: 1970–1990

The third phase (1970-90) included both decline and growth. As we have seen, the period includes the decline of the theory of international politics movement, an ambitious attempt at building a general theory of international politics (i.e. a monistic general theory often built on a positivist platform). Holsti (1971) describes the glorious aspirations of the TIP movement but spends most of his energy describing how the endeavour ended in failure and demise. Had Holsti waited five to ten years, he would have been able to include the swansong of the TIP movement, Kenneth Waltz's *Theory of International Politics* (1979), a book which, especially in the US, elevated neorealism to its prominent status as one of the premier theoretical orientations and, for better or worse, as a general theory of international politics.

Disciplinary growth includes a broad range of developments. With the demise of TIP, theorizing widened in terms of perspectives, thereby becoming a more pluralist undertaking. The scattered idea of a hegemonic (realist) paradigm was replaced by a gradual recognition of multiple theoretical traditions, each a mansion of a plurality of theoretical perspectives. Initiatives followed to bring back the international political economy tradition and thereby a range of IPE theoretical perspectives (Strange, 1970). The IPE tradition includes Marxist perspectives, which in the west experienced a comeback during the 1970s and elsewhere turned out to have been a more constant strand of theorizing. The revival of normative issues, to some degree triggered by the Vietnam War, brought back political philosophy and thus IPT (Ball, 1995). Within the liberal theoretical tradition, theorizing was initiated with renewed energy, producing transnational theory (Kaiser, 1969; 1971; Keohane and Nye, 1971), interdependence theory (Keohane and Nye, 1977; 1987) and regional integration theory (Haas, Nye, Schmitter). The English School emerged as a distinct though somewhat diverse tradition, characterized by two main currents of thought.

The failure of TIP enabled a levelling of theorizing in the sense of not only engaging in theorizing at the level of theoretical traditions or paradigms but also making use of the option of theory building at the mid-range level. With the widening and levelling of theorizing, it became a challenge to understand the inter-paradigm debates, that is, the distinctive features of contending traditions, their fault-lines as well as shared features (Banks, 1985). In fact, this trend was a continuation of Wight's critique of the two-school approach and his introduction of the *via media* or rationalist tradition.[4] It also followed Susan Strange's (1970) successful plea to reintroduce IPE as part of the IR portfolio, not to mention Helga Haftendorn and Coral Bell's efforts to raise the profile of the subdiscipline foreign policy studies. Finally, the gradual introduction of the positivism versus postpositivism axis of meta-theoretical reflection upgraded the analytical perspectives on theoretical interaction.

The pronounced and easily detected subdisciplinary developments triggered new endeavours in theorizing, yet these endeavours were bounded by the questions theorists highlighted within IR's subdisciplines, whether within economics, security studies or diplomacy. The period also saw the research-teaching nexus consolidated, not least due to the general growth of institutions of higher education. New universities were keen to demonstrate their added value and were therefore open to including 'new' disciplines such as IR; their openness stood in stark contrast to traditional, well-established universities (Smith, 1985).

The arrival of meta-theoretical reflections is probably the key indicator of substantive theorizing having reached a mature level, and the two decades did see the first arrivals (e.g. Reynolds, 1973). The period also witnessed the arrival of the first comparative studies of disciplinary trajectories, thus vindicating the idea that the discipline does not develop along a universal avenue but instead displays variation along different themes and geographies.

In general, the key feature of the period is that theorizing became more embedded in the activities of the IR community – unevenly embedded, that is. Moreover, the growth in terms of theoretical reflection resulted in a decline of the inferiority complex that Fox was concerned about in the late 1950s. Instead, it was during the third phase that the discipline became mature and increasingly defined by its theories.

Phase 4: 1990–2013

The fourth phase can be seen as both an extension and an extinction of the former phase. In many ways, the trending 1990s continued and brought more of the same. Year after year, scholars go to conferences searching for something new – only to find more of the same. The rationalism–constructivism axis remains an important fault-line, perhaps because it is essentially about the degree to which templates drawn from Economics or Sociology should inform our investigations. The extinction aspect refers partly to the trend of introducing hypo-time in IR, that is, the examination of free-floating data-informed hypotheses (the degeneration of positivism) and partly to advocacy time, that is, the instrumental use (or abandonment) of theory to promote what ought to happen. The natural consequence of critical theorizing is that, when the abandonment of a given theory is on the agenda, the predictable analytical move is to deploy Robert Cox (1981) – and, on this basis, to argue either that it is a problem-solving theory (and thus dismissible) or that the theory legitimizes a given policy (to which the critical scholars happen not to subscribe). If one is ready to go beyond this kind of binary thinking, it would be an option to acknowledge that both types of theory have their legitimate functions. Horkheimer's version of critical theory has soon been around for 90 years and has demonstrated its value but that also applies to so-called problem-solving theory.

There are four major exceptions to the more-of-the-same trend. The first is the perpetual attack on and abandonment of the 'isms'. This comes in three varieties – eclecticism, a new ism, and atheoretical hypothesis testing – and is seemingly triggered by a shared dissatisfaction with the increasingly ceremonial and unfruitful deadlocks the ism-informed analysis can generate. The praise of eclecticism involves a case-centric approach and an instrumental application of theories. The argument is that a given case is best understood if its analysis is informed by multiple theories. The challenge is to secure a controlled multiplicity and to avoid a hotpot approach (Sil and Katzenstein, 2010). The most pointed attack on isms of all orientations highlighted how isms turned into articles of faith (Lake, 2011). Abandoning the master-slave relationship between theory and method, the methodists became so impressed by methodological hair-splitting activities and the endless search for ever more and bigger datasets that theoretical reflection became a task too far, and the isms were the first casualty of this project.

The second exception is the emerging trend of arguing that the origin of theory and analysis matter, not least its west-centric attack on 'western' theory. While awareness of the limits of western scholarship is an old-style discovery (Russell, 1936; Wight, 1964; Bull, 1972; Puchala, 1997), the scale of the contemporary attack is unprecedented. It may perhaps be surprising, but the 1979 Islamic Revolution in Iran seems to have been a triggering factor. Soon after, intellectuals and scholars in the Middle East began raising doubts about the applicability or desirability of western concepts and theories, arguing that the Islamic world should be understood on its own terms and that more than one road leads to modernity. Segments of scholars within Middle East Studies picked up the idea and, boosted by Edward Said's (1978) notion of orientalism and Samir Amin's (1989) notion of Eurocentrism, the critique eventually spilled over into the study of international relations.

The popular idea in the 1980s and 1990s that there is a US disciplinary hegemony, sometimes extended to an Anglo-American hegemony, prompted an interest in anti-hegemonic moves. If the discipline represented a western project, it should be either abandoned or globalized. Its theoretical portfolio should be thoroughly reconsidered, if not dumped and replaced with that which the thus far unheard or silenced voices from the Global South have to say. For a discipline that is partly defined by its theories, an abandonment of such magnitude would obviously be a fatal blow. Paradoxically, the attack has its epicentre in two coastal regions: the west coast of Europe (including an island off the coast) and the American east coast, which is about as western as it gets. The cherished eastern agency is as absent from post-western IR studies as it was during colonial times. Moreover, the impact of space, Mannheim and Morgenthau's *Standortgebundenheit*, only seems to apply to 'western' theory. Finally, the attack strikingly resembles arguments within the Middle East orientalism-in-reverse group (al-Azm, 1981; Achcar, 2008).

The third exception is the process whereby the fashion changed, or, in concrete terms, how scholars replaced a focus on norms with a focus on practices. Whereas the 1990s and the 2000s were (sociological) norms decades, producing an avalanche of constructivist studies (for an assessment, see Finnemore and Sikkink, 2001), the 2010s became a (sociological) practices decade, triggered by Emanuel Adler and Vincent Pouliot's (2011) path-breaking article on international practices, from the very beginning a standard reference for a sizeable segment within the IR community with an interest in sociological approaches to the study of international relations. Once the term 'practices' was out in the open, it became one of the key centres of attention.

The fourth exception is the growing interest in non-state ontologies. What I have in mind here are three different initiatives. First, Peter Katzenstein's initiative to bring back the notion of civilization, particularly his efforts to make the concept an analytical one. During the early days of the discipline, Arnold Toynbee was the premier scholar to employ the term and he used it in his theory of international relations (Navari, 2000). The term almost disappeared during the grand (self-)shaming of western civilization, only to reappear with Katzenstein's eminent trilogy (2009; 2011; 2012; for a contrast, see Huntington, 1993). Second, if civilization is back, so is empire, partly as an analytical concept, yet predominantly as an ideologically convenient term. The third advance is John Ruggie's (2003) research on the global public domain and the Global Compact, including corporate social responsibility, research that reflects his policy entrepreneurship as UN deputy secretary-general. The analyst of the state of the art of an art of the state became a practitioner of an art of global governance.

Phase 5: 2013 to present

A special issue of the *European Journal of International Relations*, on 'The End of International Relations Theory?' (2013), kicked off the most recent phase. It was not so much the distinct features of the special issue, such as the fact that it appeared in a Europe-based journal or that it had a deliberately provocative title; it was more that it pinpointed and represented several underlying reflective commotions in the IR community. Thus, I referred earlier to Lake's war on the 'evil' theoretical paradigms, an approach that mirrors (in direction but not in form) advances in eclectic theoretical reflection (Sil and Katzenstein, 2010). Moreover, the tendency within American academia, described so well by Mearsheimer and Walt (2013), has been to downplay theoretical reflection and to replace it with bland hypothesis testing, mixed with superficial conceptualization. The special issue somehow epitomized ongoing efforts to leave IR's theoretical traditions behind and to replace them with whatever theoretical reflection authors happen to fancy or, alternatively, subscribe to an atheoretical stance that offers analytical conceptual lenses that might better guide us through encounters with the complexities of praxis (Kratochwil, 2018). It is hardly any wonder that these relatively recent theoretical (and non-theoretical) developments and trajectories imply diverse views about what the discipline is or should be, including the existential questions of whether it *is* and whether it *should be*. It is probably too early to tell how recent developments will have an impact on the power politics among disciplines, that is, a distinct form of politics that is the topic of the next section.

Power politics among disciplines

For scientific disciplines, theoretical reflection is one of the most important sources of legitimacy. It is one of the gold standards. The sources of legitimacy should always be appreciated, especially within the human sciences, the fate of which seems to be always challenged and their legitimacy always questioned. Apart from cases where human science scholars inflict harm on their own disciplines, other sciences and their disciplines are keen to challenge the human sciences as legitimate systems of knowledge production.[5] Numerous universities have downgraded the social sciences or subsumed them within business schools. The publisher SAGE has initiated a rescue programme aimed at highlighting the value of the human sciences. It is of little comfort here and now that things were also difficult in the past.

For a discipline under construction such as IR during the 1950s, legitimacy was obviously of utmost importance and theory came to play an important role, namely to counter inferiority complexes. W.T.R. Fox (1967) contemplated a dream scenario in which 'the international relations scholar would feel less inferior if he had a body of propositions as difficult for his colleagues to understand and evaluate as some of theirs are for him' (p. 82). With an eye for the problems that concerned Fox, Hedley Bull understood that scholars became sensitive to the underdeveloped state of theoretical work in their own subject by comparison with that of other branches of the social sciences. In some measure, what underlay this sensitivity was the academic inferiority complex that was affecting all the social sciences other than economics. … and that the way to overcome this neglect was to borrow or adapt the tools that appeared to have yielded results in other disciplines. (Bull, 1972: 40)

In the context of the role of theory in the politics among disciplines, it is worthwhile noting that Bull and Morgenthau interpret the accomplishments of the realists markedly differently. For Bull, realists enjoyed a brief heyday in the 1940s and 1950s, especially because they provided an antidote to the political utopian idealism of the 1930s. However, Bull was not impressed by their theoretical accomplishments. They produced 'powerful polemical essays', but 'not even the best of the "realist" writings can be said to have achieved a high standard of theoretical refinement' (Bull, 1972: 39). By contrast, Morgenthau blames the interwar reformists for the underdeveloped state of theoretical affairs. 'As long as such a negative orientation toward the nature of international relations and foreign policy persisted, it was both intellectually and morally impossible to deal in a theoretical, that is, an objective, systematic manner, with problems of international relations' (Morgenthau, 1962: 69).

In a sense, both Bull and Morgenthau lost their respective arguments. Did they not warn against rational approaches to international politics? Did the discipline in the US not turn to the rational natural sciences for inspiration, analytical tools and methodologies, such as cybernetics, systems research and game theory? In many ways, the 'rationalist turn' aimed at a discipline that would perform better in the zero-sum games for funding and staff. Hence, the first massive wave of searching for legitimacy outside the human sciences took place in the country where, for some, even the term 'social science' carried connotations of socialism, hence the alternative term 'behavioural sciences'. The creation of modernist social science included IR (Bevir, 2017; Bevir and Hall, 2017). By the late 1960s, the grandiose experiment with the upgrading of IR had failed. While the prime outlet for behavioural studies, the *Journal of Conflict Resolution*, survived, no general theory of international politics had been established and no platform for comparative foreign policy research had been created (Aron, 1967; Holsti, 1971; 1985; Bull, 1972; Hoffmann, 1977; Carlsnaes, 2015).

Is there more to be said about the role of theory in the politics among disciplines? Quite a bit more. This account applies to North America and a few outlets. In the rest of the world the value of theoretical reflection is less pronounced. In some places, the value of public intellectuals and public philosophies is considerably higher than theoretical reflection. However, the modernist turn was, despite its universalist credentials, not universal. As Bevir and Hall (2017; see also 2020; Hall and Bevir 2014) point out in passing, the UK experience was different from the North American; and, one could add, most other sites were also different. For the discipline as practised throughout the world, the 'theoretical turn' was a disruption that took part of the IR community down its own distinct avenue. This places Hoffmann's 'only in America' in an intriguing perspective. It did not mean that the discipline developed *only* in America and nowhere else; rather, it means that the discipline followed a distinct trajectory in America and that the patterns of disciplinary growth fell out of sync and took different directions. Thus, it is time to relativize theory as a gold standard. It may apply particularly to North America and parts of Europe but not so much to other parts of the world.

Finally, theory has an important function in processes of subdiscipline formation, and these processes may in turn have an impact on the politics among disciplines. The mushrooming of IR subdisciplines has been remarkable. While war studies at some point morphed into defence studies, and scholars in the field of study triggered at some point a process by which they carved out security studies, complete with an impressive set of security theories. Similar features characterize the differentiation between international society and international system, each concept equipped with its own set of theories. Finally, studies of globalization and global governance sparked distinct collections of theories. The stability of subdisciplines depends to some degree on their ability to generate theories. In this respect, the contrast between security studies and regionalization studies is remarkable, the former being well ahead of the latter.[6] In addition to relations between discipline and subdisciplines, there is the option of turning

IR into a meta-discipline, an option Buzan and Little suggested while also issuing a warning about power politics. They claim that if IR does not reinvent itself as a meta-discipline,

> it risks being outflanked on its own terrain by intellectual expeditions from other disciplines, and losing the holistic perspective that should be its main strength. As we have shown, many of the disciplinary borders that surround IR are permeable if approached in the right way. That openness is an opportunity for the discipline, but also a danger if IR allows its natural territory to be colonised by other disciplines. (Buzan and Little, 2001: 38–9)

Conclusion

If disciplines have a spine, then theoretical reflection is clearly part of it. The conclusion of the chapter is, first, that theory performs a range of functions in the practice of constituting and reproducing the discipline. By upgrading knowledge from the particular to the general (with several levels in between), the act of theorizing synthesizes knowledge. It follows that the distinction between intellectual and practical functions is important if we want to understand the uneven distribution of efforts at theorizing international relations or aspects of these relations.

The second conclusion is that IR is a dynamic discipline, which means that theory, the meanings of theory for the discipline and the functions of theory all change over time. As noted earlier, scholars made the first references to theory during the 1930s, after which they took theory through some profound twists and turns. In order for IR to remain (or to become) relevant, the function of triggering questions for empirical research was adapted to changing circumstances – to world politics on the move. Theories capable of asking relevant questions were in demand, for instance, questions about the emerging European integration process, decolonization, nuclear weapons, globalization and cyberspace. Given that disciplines are or should be defined by their guiding research questions, the function of proposing questions should come as no surprise, especially given the important role theory plays in providing a *raison d'être* and legitimacy for disciplines. Both Fox and Bull pointed to an early inferiority complex as a motivating factor for building a portfolio of IR theories. With the contemporary specialized vocabulary, Fox's dream scenario has come true – yet not always for the better.

Finally, theory building has a role to play in the power politics among disciplines. It was the challenges felt by IR scholars after the Second World War that prompted an increase in endeavours at theorizing, at least in parts of the world. In other parts of the world, legitimacy was found in IR scholars' engagement in representing or challenging public philosophies about world politics and the desirable or likely prospective role of their own country in the international order.[7] With reference to the power politics among disciplines, the processes of subdiscipline formation play an important role in the constitution and growth of IR, and should not be overlooked.

5

What is Disciplinary Diversity?

Introduction

In recent decades, diversifiers have repeatedly made calls to move beyond hegemony and towards more diversity in IR. There is no apparent end to how diverse the discipline should be, nor any end to how diverse diversity can be. With its plurality of theoretical traditions, myriads of methodologies to serve the theories, a dozen subdisciplines, various regional disciplinary cultures, and its straddling of the social sciences and the humanities, IR is actually as diverse as it gets. Moreover, in reality there is no hegemony. Based on comprehensive empirical studies, Helen Turton (2015) concludes against conventional wisdom, that (American) hegemony is first and foremost an imagined state of affairs. Likewise, May Darwich et al (Darwich et al, 2020; Darwich and Kaarbo, 2020) document how IR scholars in the Arab world teach IR in a non-hegemonic fashion. Others point out that Japan has its own configuration of research traditions (Inoguchi and Bacon, 2001). Olubukola Adesina (2020) shows how scholars based in Africa offer important concepts, theories and wider perspectives that do not reflect a supposedly hegemonic 'Centre'; indeed, she points to the observation that some of the supposedly western ideas originate in Africa.[1] Hence, both the widespread prescriptions offered as well as the hegemony 'diagnosis' would appear to be resting on shaky foundations.

Nonetheless, diversity remains an issue, and a contested one at that. Whereas some believe the discipline to be far too diverse, counting diversity as a threat to coherence, discipline or 'monotheism' of sorts, others believe the discipline is much too short on diversity – at least diversity as they understand it. The present chapter offers an invitation to consider a possible dispute settlement. As any such mediation begins with an understanding of the positions of the contending parties and their stakes as well as their identity issues, I first outline what Party A – 'diversity is a threat' – tends to argue, followed by Party B's – 'ever more diversity' – arguments. It is likely that one of the parties will protest this procedure, claiming that their understanding of diversity should be superior or even enjoy monopoly. However, if granted superiority the mediation would fail even before it started. In Kenneth Thompson's words, "Only the tyranny of intellectual life would be served by installing one approach as pre-eminent" (Thompson 1955: 746). Thirdly, I outline the principles (but not the specificities) of a dispute settlement that addresses the main issues of contestation. I am well aware that dispute settlement might be a futile enterprise, not least because the contending parties may use diversity instrumentally to polish their professional or personal identities.

Indeed, the chapter is very much about processes of identity formation within IR. I argue that these processes represent a present and real danger caused by three intertwined factors. First, whereas the discipline according to a (particularly in the US and parts of Europe) widespread self-image is seen as merely a subset of political science, the discipline is worldwide increasingly practised beyond political science and, as we saw in Chapter 2, both within the social sciences and the humanities. The self-image in the US is sustained by institutional structures within universities but these structures do not constrain US-based IR scholars from voting with their feet, that is, predominantly opting for ISA conventions and not for political science association alternatives. The liberation from political science and other 'prisons' (Rosenberg, 2016) enables a diversity that would be unthinkable within the confines of Political Science (or Law or Economics). Second, numbers matter. Given that a relatively limited number of scholars practised in the field for a large part of the 20th century, it is a field of study that has attracted increasing numbers of scholars and students in the last 40 years. While this increasing number of scholars is most welcome, it seems to imply a diversity that has 'gone wild' to some degree. Professional socialization has been lagging behind growth. Third, scholars often reduce their accounts of the discipline to accounts concerning contributions in English or from the United States or, more broadly, an unspecified 'centre', the 'west' or, more recently, the 'Global North'. Current efforts to globalize the discipline tend occasionally to destabilize long-held yet parochial narratives about the origins and growth of the discipline over the course of the 20th century. In other words, we have numerous histories of the discipline pretending to be global but we do not yet have a genuinely global history of the origins and trajectories of the discipline. Combined, the three factors – configuration, numbers and globalization – are bound to have an impact on disciplinary identities.

The topic of the chapter is thus on the contemporary agenda of academic politics in the discipline, but it can also and should be seen in historical context. Indeed, the 'discipline and diversity' theme is a classic within the discipline. It has been discussed as long as the discipline has existed. It is therefore well-known that the theme can be presented both as a dilemma and as a positive sum game. The latter option informs the section entitled a truly diverse discipline, a section that briefly outlines how the diversity-discipline dialectics shaped the discipline. The chapter, thus, presents a few but important ideas about diversity and the discipline of IR. In order to stimulate reflection and discussion, I present my critical observations and arguments in a bolder fashion than usual.

Diversity as a threat

Imagine a joint-venture state-of-the-art analysis conducted during the years after the Second World War. In a retrospective perspective, analysts would look at approaches employed, accomplishments in terms of studies produced, theoretical advances made, community building, and the like. The analysis would also include prescriptions about the way forward. With the help of articles and books published at the time, we know that the imagined team of authors did not manage to produce a consensus report (Morgenthau, 1946;

Wolfers, 1947; Fox, 1949; Thompson 1952; Zimmern, 1953). However, the publications do suggest that it was not uncommon to conclude that what happened during the interwar years should not continue. They considered the study of international relations as too much of an interdisciplinary fleamarket, a dispersed field of study, and conclude either that an autonomous discipline is called for or that the study of international relations finds a spot within the disciplines of Law, Political Science or History. According to their analysis of the interwar years, diversity is a threat and discipline is called for. Kenneth W. Thompson is keenly aware of resistance among historians and political scientists to the idea of IR as a distinct discipline yet he also shows no mercy in his assessment, 'No serious student would presume to claim that the study of international relations had arrived at the stage of an independent academic discipline' (Thompson 1952: 433).

During the following years, the diversity-as-threat argument continues to pop up. Diversity is seen as not the good but the bad guy, associated with fragmentation and disarray, causing a dividing discipline. Scholars taking this stance regret diversity and think there is too much of it. The following illustrative examples in this section show how different scholars share a negative perspective on diversity yet represent different concerns. A prominent scholar, Kal Holsti (1985), has concerns about theoretical diversity and argues that the proliferation of more and more theories regrettably has resulted in the disappearance of a disciplinary core. By shifting away from a focus on the relations between states and issues of war and peace, Holsti argues that IR has gone astray. Indeed, the opening sentence of Holsti's *The Dividing Discipline* announces with much regret that 'international theory is in a state of *disarray*'. Hence, feeling a threat and experiencing a dividing discipline, Holsti pleads for discipline and outlines the main dimensions of it. With *Along the Road of International Theory* (2001), Holsti brings his argument into the 21st century and, in sarcastic prose, he describes how instead of advances he observes multiple step in the wrong direction.

Perceptions of diversity as a threat do not only concern theoretical diversity and they are not merely things of the past, dated material we can dispose and forget about. According to David Lake (2011), diversity at the level of paradigmatic perspectives is a threat, an unwarranted diversity, the isms are evil and should be abandoned.[2]

Instead, a hegemonic 'consensus' theoretical orientation should be adopted. It is primarily the incommensurability of the isms that makes Lake uncomfortable, a discomfort he shares with a considerable segment within the IR community; that is, those who feel uncomfortable whenever facing non-monistic orientations. With Kuhn's (1962/1970) famous book on paradigm shifts, the incommensurability theorem got a boost but as acknowledged by Kuhn himself, Ludwik Fleck (1935) introduced the idea almost three decades earlier. Thus, while the choice of Lake (2011) might be seen as random selection, it is illustrative of not only the numerous scholars who have lost appetite for theoretical paradigms but also those who have a hard time accepting that incommensurability is a condition we need to accept and learn to live with.

Scholars do not always forward the diversity as threat argument at the level of theory or paradigms. Occasionally, scholars employ it in a much more specific fashion. Two examples suffice to illustrate what I have in mind. The first example is Robert Jarvis. Jarvis (2000) does not aim at theoretical or paradigmatic diversity. He aims at defending the discipline against postmodernism. While he acknowledges and appreciates the diversity of theoretical approaches, there are limits. Thus, he takes issue with the premises of poststructural and postmodern scholarship as practised in IR. As such, his book is among the most comprehensive studies of the unwarranted impact of certain features of the Third Debate. Jarvis simply considers the diversity sponsored by poststructural and postmodern approaches a threat to the discipline. Subsequently, Jarvis zooms in with a chapter *Identity Politics, Postmodern Feminisms, and International Theory: Questioning the "New" Diversity in International Relations* in which he spots a new type of diversity threat and, as the chapter title suggests, a type he is highly critical of.

The second example is Ann Tickner (1998) who, when commenting on Kal Holsti states that, the '[c]elebration of difference is troubling to many mainstream scholars who, in Kal Holsti's words, see a "discipline in disarray"'. As we saw earlier, Tickner has a point, but the scope of 'troubling' is wider than she presents it. The problem is that non-mainstream scholars also tend to find celebration of difference troubling, so while they share the sense of something being troubling (they tend to prefer the word 'problematic'), their trouble is of less consequence, exactly because they are not mainstream.[3] They call for the closure of theoretical orientations to which they do not subscribe. Moreover, they refuse to discuss the relative merits of different theoretical orientations. Finally, they reject the relevance of others' assessments of their own theoretical platform.

These examples focus on theoretical and paradigmatic diversity, but, as argued in Chapter 3, disciplinary diversity has a much wider scope than that while also acknowledging Hoffmann's (1959) observation that a 'fleamarket is not a discipline' (p. 348).

Ever more diversity?

As mentioned in the introduction to this chapter, there have been ever more suggestions to create a more inclusive and diverse IR, including calls to 'open up spaces', promote 'unheard voices', construct an 'ever wider field', extend the 'subject matter' ever more and thorough critiques of 'narrow understandings'. The doubts and concerns about the boundaries of the discipline have been so constant and frequent that they constitute the data material for an entire article, 'Discipline Admonished: On International Relations Fragmentation and the Disciplinary Politics of Stocktaking' (Kristensen, 2016). Without such calls and their successful reception, the discipline would not be the pluralist and diverse enterprise it is anno 2021.

However, the calls for diversity come in two different groups: one group that aims at extending the discipline, making it dynamic and responsive to new challenges, and a second group that uses diversity as an excuse to undermine and eventually get rid of discipline. The interwar years witnessed the launch of the first group, because questions about international economics, nationalism and international society soon complemented a narrow war and peace agenda. Moreover, we saw in Chapter 1, how the English School in the 1950s extended the discipline's two-school approach (liberalism and realism) and how, during the 1970s, IPE and IPT was reintegrated in the discipline thereby making it a more diverse discipline. If we look beyond the Anglo-American tradition (see Wolfers and Martin, 1956; Bell, 2009), which characterized the years of Cold War and which critics of the discipline insist on reproducing (only to deconstruct it), we see an even more diverse discipline, ranging from for instance sociological IR in Continental Europe to distinct IR traditions in Japan. In this context, we should not forget the reawakening of the Marxist tradition with its focus on class and capital. Subsequently it was suggested that international relations has a gender dimension and the 1970s class and capitalism perspectives were replaced by gender perspectives, especially the perspectives of one of the genders. Calls for diversity did not only reflect a dynamic discipline – the high and low tide and the shifting closures and bringing-back-in pleas, calls also became a tool to claim a home in the disciplines.

The second group is an altogether different enterprise, heterogeneous in its claims yet sharing the aspiration to employ diversity as a means to sacrifice the discipline. The following four examples show the determination to opt out of IR and into a 'diverse' field.

First, at the level of semantics, some scholars have strong reservations about the term 'IR discipline', pointing out the prominent role of, for instance, IPE or IPT which they consider excluded from IR. Hence, they prefer 'international studies' or take processes of globalization into account, thus preferring 'global studies'. My first observation is thus that IR is a contested and challenged enterprise, even at the semantic level.

Second, brewed during the 1980s yet experiencing momentum at the dawn of the 1990s, postmodernist and poststructuralist critique targeted the Enlightenment, science, rationalism, modernity and much more (Ashley and Walker, 1990b). In this grand context, the critique of disciplines is perhaps best seen as collateral damage. But damaging nonetheless and, significantly, producing a meaning of diversity that previously did not make it to any position of consequence. However, this time things went differently. Jarvis (2000) summarizes the outcome: 'History, in other words, is to be rewritten, or at least written from the perspective of those who have not written it before: women, people of color, gays and lesbians, indigenous peoples, and so forth' (p. 20). In short, as Jarvis highlighted in a different context (Jarvis, 2001), identity politics enters the discipline, not in order to make it a more diverse discipline but in order to destroy it. In the language of centre-periphery, the challenge did not emerge from the periphery but from the centre. In many ways, it was an internal western affair.

Third, the second group comprises more than postmodernists and poststructuralists. For instance political theorist Chris Brown (2001) who points out how

> the dominant mode of thinking in the modern discipline is profoundly cosmopolitan ... the intellectual predispositions of the American discipline are universalist, committed to denying the privileging of any particular national viewpoint – indeed to denying the very idea that a national viewpoint could have any intellectual validity (p. 216) ... [and, moreover, if] we truly wish to promote diversity in international thought, it may be that a crucial first step will be to contribute to the work of dismantling 'International Relations' as an academic discipline. (p. 218)

In Brown's perspective, the modern academic discipline is an American discipline and the precondition for genuine diversity is that we dismantle the discipline. While Brown does not employ the centre-periphery dichotomy. It seems to be the case that the 'centre' has to go for non-cosmopolitan international thought to appear. Calls for decentring or decolonizing the discipline point in the same direction though characterized by even less specification about the telos.

Fourth, some aim at dissolving what there is of discipline instead praising IR as an interdisciplinary field. Pami Aalto et al (2011) present International Studies as a wide, plural and inherently interdisciplinary field of research, a field of study where it is possible to draw freely on all relevant disciplines. For the IR as an interdisciplinary-field-of-study position, diversity is built into the definition of the field and therefore almost guaranteed. Instead of a firm disciplinary hand, analysts prefer a free hand. Such a field is consuming and integrating knowledge, but one should not expect the field of study to be a source of inspiration for scholars within other disciplines. According to Buzan and Little (2001), IR has failed as an intellectual project, in as much as those working in other disciplines generally find little inspiration; our imports exceed our exports, so to speak. The interdisciplinary-field-of-study position sees little need for discipline in the sense of cultivating an integrated approach within the boundaries of a discipline.

The different orientations are clearly linked to different conceptions of what a discipline is or should be. Moreover, the different conceptions of IR have markedly different implications for the relationship between discipline and diversity.

Settling the dispute?

Dispute settlement is a process about reaching an agreement that may not be perfect or fair but is nonetheless acceptable. To arrive at an agreement, communication or dialogue is necessary. There are different kinds of dialogue (Jørgensen and Valbjørn, 2012), however, and some have a better chance of producing agreement than others. Some dialogues are eristic, which means that their function is not to argue and possibly reach a consensus[4] but rather to consolidate existing positions and enforce identities; for this reason eristic dialogues are characterized more by yelling than arguing. Diversity dialogues occasionally seem to be eristic, and the search for possible dispute settlement is futile in such cases, as one or both parties make a priority of using the dialogue to fortify their position. It follows that the proposal aims at those who are willing to engage in non-eristic dialogue, perhaps even in a reflexive dialogue. As mentioned in the introduction to this chapter, it focuses on six principles that could be part of a settlement, thus leaving specificities for future deliberations.

The first principle is that diversity means a range of different things. It may appear banal, but it challenges those who want to monopolize the meaning of diversity, for instance claiming that the chapter is not about diversity but about a fragmented discipline. To unpack the diverse meanings of diversity, it is helpful to consider synonyms and antonyms. In relation to synonyms, it makes sense to include terms such as 'variety', 'assortment', 'mixture', 'mix', 'melange', 'range', 'array', 'medley' and 'multiplicity'. In the context of IR, things are no different: diversity can mean multiple different things. Antonyms to diversity are 'hegemony', 'dominance', 'conventions', 'orthodoxy' and 'mainstream'. Calls to globalize the discipline, for instance, often employ the notion of geographical diversity to reduce a hegemony or dominance that is claimed to be American, western or Eurocentric (see Chapter 7).

The second principle is that contemporary calls for diversity tend to be based more on normative preferences than on empirical studies. It is thus predicable that diversity would be a problem if those making pleas neglect the actually existing diversity. A problem of similar magnitude is the prevalent selection bias: select literature with an origin in 'the west' only to conclude that it is predominantly 'western'.

Diversity often refers to inclusion (i.e. the opposite of exclusion). From this perspective, the discipline should be more inclusive of non-western concepts, theories and intellectual traditions. The third principle is that this use of diversity represents a normative view that is underpinned by a biased analysis of the concepts employed by the members of the IR community.

While somewhat similar to inclusion, diversity also refers to theoretical and methodological pluralism, such as multiple theoretical perspectives (Ferguson, 2015). The fourth principle is that this kind of diversity should be acknowledged and not dismissed. This is a different way of saying that 'boxing' individuals, schools, strands and traditions may be heuristically useful but is also exceptionally harmful to actually existing diversity. As we have seen, some scholars occasionally see diversity as an unwarranted feature of the discipline, one associated with fragmentation and disarray (Holsti, 1985).

Fifth, 'discipline' is a term with dual meanings. Even a casual consultation of online dictionaries suggest as much, and a deep dive into Foucault's work confirms the dual nature of discipline. In the present context, I will skip such a lengthy Foucauldian excursion, instead highlighting the two sides of the discipline coin, as a branch of knowledge and as a means of socialization.

On the one hand, discipline refers to a branch of scientific knowledge, typically one studied or produced at institutions of higher education (see Chapter 3). Even a shortlist includes several synonyms and enables a fair amount of flexibility in interpreting what a discipline is. The problems begin when tacit understandings and implicit or explicit *connotations* take over from *definitions*, and when preferences or symbolic meanings are implicitly or explicitly loaded into concepts. Three random examples serve to illustrate the problem. Leonie Holthaus (2020) seems to believe that liberal internationalism is an exclusively British orientation and that British liberal internationalists constructed Nazi Germany as a foe. Scholars in favour of decentring practices (Nayak and Selbin, 2013) believe that the IR discipline is a western invention and that it ought to be decentred. Felix Grenier (2015) believes that the version of the discipline within which he was trained *is* the discipline.

On the other hand, 'discipline' refers to the practice of training people to follow or obey rules or a code of behaviour, sometimes using punishment to correct disobedience. According to the fifth principle, discipline in this sense cannot be avoided. The existence of multiple synonyms suggests that we are dealing with a complex term. When we characterize discipline as regulation, it is possible – indeed necessary – to examine the role of and *the degree of discipline* in the IR discipline. This may sound awfully negative to some ears, perhaps because discipline is occasionally associated with punishment. However, is teaching IR to students, undergraduates and graduates alike, not about training and a moulding of the mind and character to bring about desired outcomes? For instance:

- Training an open mind is often preferred to training a closed mind, at least in some parts of the world.
- In university teaching, critical thought is often the first step, because students arrive with all sorts of world-views, some of which are not up to our professional standards. It is part of our job to teach students about professional standards and, it seems to me that even the most libertarian-minded scholars do so.
- In introductory IR courses, do we not introduce a particular, well-known, consensually foundational literature? While the content of the foundational literature tends to differ from course to course, the idea is that a basic body of literature represents the discipline, including its mythologies about beginnings and its theoretical traditions and theories.
- Are PhD programmes not designed to socialize doctoral students to adhere to what is perceived to be professional standards and conventions? Such processes of socialization require a lot of discipline.

In short, discipline is an essential part of teaching. Moreover, everyday practices document numerous persistent attempts by scholars to regulate the activities of colleagues and thereby the discipline. Two examples will suffice. Robert Keohane's (1989) presidential address in 1988, in which he aimed at regulating the upcoming 'reflective' (constructivist) turn. Richard Ashley and R.B.J. Walker (1990a; 1990b), as well as others, have protested the attempted discipline, yet the most successful branch of constructivism took notice and eventually benefited from Keohane's intervention (Katzenstein, 1996; Katzenstein et al, 1998; Finnemore and Sikkink, 2001). The second example concerns security studies. Whenever a scholar aims to understand contemporary security threats and presents a paper on the topic, someone predictably protests using the terms 'securitization', 'Eurocentric', 'white' or 'male', each of which is designed to discipline the paper presenter.[5] My point is that, while 'discipline' may have negative connotations, we all practise it all the time and in both individual and institutionalized ways (e.g. we practise peer review, which is an increasingly well-established institution within academia around the world). Likewise, as scholars, we are usually *objects* of discipline. Instances of discipline include departmental, university or ministerial regulations, peer review, citation and other statistical metrics, accreditation agencies and so forth.

Finally, while diversity is a key feature of a dynamic discipline, no discipline can be unlimited in its inclusion of subject matters or questions asked. In other words, disciplines have boundaries, which means that at some point a given study is no longer a study just within the discipline but also a study within one or other of the many other disciplines, for instance Mathematics, Biology or Literary Studies. It is very rare to come across scholars who argue in this fashion, Robert Jackson (2000), however, is an exception, reasoning that he cannot see why X, Y and Z are not something other than IR. The implication of the principle is that individual scholars who for various reasons do not want to contribute to the IR discipline have a wide range of alternatives. They have ample opportunities to follow their own agendas.

A truly diverse discipline

Every new generation tends to claim that world politics and economics is more complex than ever before, that technological change has been unprecedented and that new realities require new thinking or at least a reconsideration of conventional wisdom. While part of the claim can be reduced to a new generation facing a complex world (who has never been overwhelmed by such a situation?), the claim also reflects real game changers in operation in the real world. Thus, the 19th century industrial revolution in Europe – a real-world process – triggered a wave of geopolitical thinking (see Deudney, 2000) and a fundamental revolution in real warfare (Bloch, 1898). The introduction of air power during the First World War demonstrated that nation-states do not have secure 'roofs'; it was a real game changer which later, with the arrival of missile technology, would become an even better example of new realities triggering new ideas about international relations. Likewise, during most of the 1950s and beyond, scholars engaged in reflections about the Bomb, that is, the arrival and built up of an insane number of nuclear warheads. The arrival and expansion of the internet during the 1990s triggered an information explosion and an 'information age' (Nye, 2004), but it may be too early to ascertain the consequences of this for our thinking about world politics. While contemporary migration flows may be impressive, so was the exodus of Europeans during the period 1860-1914, not to speak of the migration of Chinese to south-east Asia and beyond. While the lesson is that an IR discipline that does not address changing new realities is in immediate danger of becoming a dinosaur discipline, the challenge is to identify a suitable balance between continuity and change.

The temporal dimension also demonstrates the diversity of a discipline. A dynamic discipline evolves over time, and its main characteristics in one decade are not necessarily its characteristics in the next. Many are keen to claim progress and to dump dated perspectives, implying that the latest generation always represents the superior (at least until the next) phase of epistemological progress (Lijphart, 1974). One might argue that this is a slightly arrogant approach. Certainly it is very different from Bull's (1972) more humble approach, for he simply suggested that every generation faces the challenge of sliding backwards in terms of what we know. In turn, when it comes to this challenge, where exactly are we after some 100 years of practice?

As we have seen in the previous chapters and will see in the chapters to come, variation is the name of the IR game. The subject matter varies greatly, as does the configuration of theoretical perspectives and, in turn, the questions scholars within the IR community ask about international relations and transnational affairs. Moreover, the underpinning meta-theoretical platforms vary, including historicism, positivism, social constructivism, rationalism and poststructuralism. Who is bold (or biased) enough to suggest a hierarchy of such platforms and a temporal sequencing towards ever better platforms? It would be truly ironic if, for example, poststructuralists were to claim epistemological progress over time.

With a view to the global scope of this book, I should emphasize that the variants and turns described earlier are not synchronized across space. Moreover, centre-periphery images are highly misleading, as impulses do not radiate from a designated centre, eventually to reach the most distant provinces of the global disciplinary empire. Rather, heterogeneous trajectories define the growth of the discipline. Chapter 7 is devoted to the issue of the *terroir* (i.e. terrain, space) on which IR communities cultivate their gardens.

We have previously seen how the 1954 Rockefeller Foundation-sponsored conference aimed at defining IR as a non-behaviouralist discipline built on the basis of a realist cornerstone (Guilhot, 2011). This idea worked wonderfully well in some places, such as Yale University, but had limited or no impact elsewhere. Despite the limited impact, the conference promoted diversity in a sense, because realism was selected to counter behaviouralist approaches. But diversity was also limited, because only realism was promoted as the 'normal science', chosen to be dominant, the most privileged tradition thus delegating other theoretical orientations to the margins. Hardly diversity promotion. Soon thereafter, Rockefeller also sponsored the British Committee, which would spin off the English School, thus diversifying the limited analytical options allowed by the liberalism/realism dichotomy, and sponsoring a pronounced anti-behaviouralist stance. However, 25 years passed before members of the school (triggered by Jones, 1981) realized that they actually constituted a distinct school. Without such knowledge and recognition, the English School could not appear on the radar as a major theoretical orientation, though its recognition has been characterized by variation across space. And, during the process of identity formation, the radar increasingly began to detect, for instance, the IPE and IPT traditions, the former strongly promoted by Susan Strange (1970).

Conclusion

The conclusion is that the discipline–diversity nexus has been, but does not need to be, a zero-sum game. In other words, it is not necessarily either diversity as a threat or ever more diversity. The chapter proposes a dispute settlement by outlining a way forward and suggesting that the third option shaped the actual history of the discipline.

The settlement proposal acknowledges that disciplines have virtue and that discipline may be a burden, yet discipline in the discipline is nonetheless an issue that must be repeatedly addressed and negotiated. While simply ignoring the issue is an option (the easy way out), it is an unwarranted one. We would then not be fully aware of what we are doing, why we do it and how it should be done, which can hardly be an attractive option for scholars who claim that human beings are self-reflexive beasts. So how do we want to discipline, or let me say train, future generations of students? What are the professional guidelines and standards within the discipline and what are the discipline's scholarly norms? It is for each individual scholar to determine if the guidelines, standards and norms constitute acceptable conditions, and are worthwhile standing up for or challenging or, deciding that the grass is greener elsewhere.

The settlement proposal also acknowledges that diversity has virtue. It is difficult for me to see how the expansion of the discipline in terms of theoretical perspectives can be seen as necessarily a discipline in disarray. It seems to be more a self-image of discipline in disarray. Nevertheless, diversity also poses challenges, especially regarding the attempts to define a core of the discipline or, by implication, its peripheries and boundaries. If the discipline is dynamic – and it seems to be, will be and should be – then the challenge is to define a core and disciplinary boundaries, the latter defined by means of key characteristics and an examination of the disciplinary contexts in which IR exists and develops. Discipline is also about socializing newcomers into what we believe to be the core literature, perpetually under (re)construction, because newcomers, despite or provoked by discipline, for better or worse, often have ideas of their own.[6] Moreover, 'theory' is a different word for abstract knowledge about the actors, structures and processes in international, world or global politics/economics/governance (choose your favourite expression); and, although contending perspectives have always existed, the configuration of theoretical traditions has been fairly stable over time and to some degree also across space. Should we consider it a risk or a blessing that 'after hegemony' might destabilize the traditional configurations? No matter how we approach the challenge, it is bound to be a condition in the years to come.

6

What is Community?

Introduction

Continuing to apply concepts that scholars frequently use in passing but that merit closer examination, this chapter focuses on community. However, the community in focus is not the international community or its rhetorical or other functions. Nor is it the imagined communities of nations or the communities on Scottish or Indonesian islands (Geertz, 1973; Cohen, 1989; Anderson, 1991). Instead, the chapter focuses on what William J. Goode (1957) refers to as a 'community within a community: the professions'; and, given our special interest in IR, the focus is particularly on the oft-mentioned but hardly analysed, little understood and not always appreciated community of IR scholars.

Community studies are often based on the conceptual triptych of self, other and boundary, which also seems to work for the purposes of this chapter. Given that boundaries exist between self and other, they deserve special attention. Kicking an article off with a rhetorical question, 'Should we leave behind the subfield of International Relations?', Dan Reiter (2015) weighs the pros and cons and eventually concludes that the subfield should be kept (for now), mainly because dividing the bits and pieces into more viable and worthy disciplines and fields of study would create new *boundary* problems. Anthony P. Cohen (1998) also makes boundaries a key feature of communities and, like other sociologists and social anthropologists, he examines communities in terms of a relational notion of identity: who are we? what do we want to be recognized for? and who are we not? Rather than suggesting a morphological approach or providing an outside definition of community and then measuring the degree to which a given community matches the definition, Cohen asks what community appears to mean to its members, acknowledging that appearances are often deceptive. In the words of the editor of the series in which Cohen's book was published, the project is to explore if the members of a community 'are able to infuse its culture with vitality, and to construct a symbolic community which provides meaning and identity' (Hamilton, 1998: 9). Building and reproducing an IR community is thus a massive undertaking, and, in turn, analysing the degree to which it happened and is happening is a considerable task. The sections in this chapter aim at assessing the degree and ways in which the IR community has been capable of constructing such a symbolic community and of infusing its culture with vitality. To explore the temporal and spatial characteristics and variations, the 100 years will be divided into three distinct phases: the interwar years, the Cold War years and the years of globalization.

The IR community during the interwar years

Early social experiments with national and transnational IR community building merit attention, even if the period is characterized by communities under construction. At the national level, the discipline and its sociological dimension – the communities – crystallized around an increasing number of institutions and centres. The newly created institutions gradually shaped a network of bilateral cooperative relations involving institutions in an increasingly long list of cities, including Geneva, Paris, Madrid, Lwów, New York, Milan, Berlin, Aberystwyth, Copenhagen, Oxford, Toronto, Hamburg and London. Not all institutions were situated within universities but they contributed to various degrees to the dual objective of developing the scientific study of international relations and promoting an international mind.

At the transnational level, community building began not in Europe but in the Pacific realm, with the creation in 1925 of the Institute of Pacific Relations (IPR). The institute was a liberal internationalist project, largely funded by the Rockefeller Foundation, and it became a hothouse for the organization of biennial conferences, producing a journal, *Pacific Affairs*, among other publications. In short, the IPR did what we now expect IR communities and associations to do. As Wikipedia shows,[1] by the standards of the day, the 1931 IPR conference in Shanghai was a sizeable event. Anderson (2009) explains that,

> Eschewing traditional diplomacy, non-governmental elites in a number of countries sought to organize intellectuals into regional partnerships, bypassing official state machinery, with the ultimate goal of bringing about better transnational understanding. This collection of scholars, businessmen, journalists and philanthropists centered themselves around a new international private organization, the Institute of Pacific Relations, as a vehicle to collect data and organize research on the social and economic problems confronting the Pacific region, (p. 23; see also Akami, 2001)

Hence, the IPR community valued civil society engagement in international affairs and promoting better international understanding. It was not exclusively an academic community, which meant that walls between scholars at universities and others had not yet been built. Moreover, new experiments in scholarly communication were carried out within the IPR, breaking with the tradition of long papers read at meetings and introducing confidentiality (Pemberton, 2020); today this is known as the Chatham House Rule.

The second major transnational experiment began a few years later, when the League of Nations-sponsored ISC took off, to some degree inspired by the IPR experience (Pemberton, 2020). In 1928 the ISC began its series of annual conferences. The first was held in Berlin to contribute symbolically to integrating Germany into the work of the League of Nations, and the last in Bergen in August 1939, just weeks before the outbreak of the Second World War. With its regular meetings, the ISC improved communications within the relatively small community, discussed 'current affairs' continuously and extended the networks between centres and peripheries. Thus Pemberton describes how a delegate travelled all the way from Tehran to attend the meetings that always took place in Europe. In addition to the transnational ISC activities, we should not forget the important network of national committees that supported the ISC, a network that was crucially important for the dissemination of values and (novel) ways of doing things. Between the conferences, it was mainly the national committees that contributed to shaping the community and growing the discipline.

The third experiment was a series of little-known meetings held each September in Geneva. Charles Manning (1962a) observes how,

> During most, though not the whole, of the thirties, the teachers of International Relations and of International Law were encouraged, and financially enabled, to spend their Septembers in company and often in lively argument with their confréres from a score of countries, and incidentally studying the functioning of the international institutions, at the seat of the League of Nations. (p. 353)[2]

Both the venue and topic reflect how the spirit of the meetings is the same as for the IPR and ISC, namely, an internationalism of a liberal orientation. The promotion of the 'international mind' was high on the ISC agenda, and teaching the public (or at least university students) was a main motivating factor. As Manning (1962a) points out, 'A major part of the *raison d'être* of International Relations as an academic discipline – or so in 1930 one assumed – would be as it were training a guide-dog for the blind' (p. 348).

By July 1937, Hans Morgenthau was fleeing for his life. After Germany and before leaving Europe, he had worked in Geneva, Paris and Madrid. He crossed the Atlantic and ended up, temporarily, as a lawyer in Kansas City (Morgenthau, 1984; Frei, 2001). Of significance in the present context is not his travelogue but that, since 1919, dozens of institutes of international affairs had been created in Europe and beyond. The members of the emerging IR community had institutional homes and engaged in three activities of significance for the symbolic construction of their community: (1) the formation of a transnational community; (2) experiments in secession from or complementing their root disciplines; (3) defining the values, norms and standards of the community.[3] They had become aware of other ways of doing and seeing things. Several specialists in international law morphed into international politics scholars, Hans Morgenthau, Georg Schwarzenberger and Ludwig Ehrlich being typical examples but far from the only ones.[4] Likewise, tensions could be ignited between, for instance, a historian with an interest in international themes and an IR scholar with an interest in the historical dimension of things. Complementing root disciplines is about systematically cultivating the residual aspect that can be found in most root disciplines: the international dimension. In cultivating the international dimension of their discipline, scholars gradually discovered scholars from other disciplines who also had an interest in international affairs, and began to discover linkages between diverse international dimensions.[5]

The IR community during the Cold War years

The 1940s to the 1960s

The story of the IR community during the Cold War is no rise-and-fall narrative. Quite the opposite. The modest beginnings of a transnational community during the interwar years were undermined by the UNESCO decision in 1954 to discontinue the activities of the ISC and by the new funding policies of the major charities, policies that prioritized national-level activities. Thus, all three of the major experiments in transnational IR community building experienced severe problems during the 1950s. While IPR first came to an end in 1960, it did run into serious problems, and there were no more Rockefeller Foundation-funded September meetings in Geneva. In Manning's (1962a) calculation, the association that replaced it, IPSA, did less to promote international studies over the course of 15 years than the ISC had accomplished 'in 10 or even 5 years before the War' (p. 367). With the exception of the British Coordinating Committee for International Studies (BCCIS), the fate of the ISC and the IPR national coordinating committees is largely unknown (Buzan, 2019). What is known is that the BCCIS continued to work and to organize the Bailey conferences, which were launched in 1933 and usually held biennially, before they were transformed in the mid-1970s into the annual BISA conference.

If transnational community building during the 1950s reached a nadir, national-level community building was strengthened and these communities contributed in different ways to consolidate the growth of the discipline. IR scholars began creating professional associations and catering for their discipline in national environments. The BCCIS may not have been an association but nonetheless it performed some of the functions of professional associations. South Korea and Japan were among the first to create professional associations in 1956, followed by the United States in 1959 (Moon and Kim, 2002). In other words, the organization of the community in associations began in the east, not the west. To promote the exchange of ideas and to become genuine scholarly communities, the framework conditions should include not only associations but also channels for communication. In this respect, the 1950s and 1960s witnessed a remarkable growth in the number of specialized journals (e.g. *Foreign Affairs, International Affairs, Kokusai-seiji, World Politics, International Relations, Cooperation and Conflict, Co-Existence, Soviet Studies, JCMS: Journal of Common Market Studies*).

In terms of the IR community values, it is significant that the community is typically considered to consist of both scholars and diplomats. The Bailey conferences were always attended by officials from the Foreign Office and occasionally from the Ministry of Defence. Scholars generally appreciated the presence of diplomats. Those initiating the creation of the ISA also valued the presence of diplomats, which was reflected in the profile of the conferences (Teune, 1982). In other words, the dynamics professionalization had yet to push practitioners (officials) out of the (mixed) community.

Second, the secession-synthesis process continued, the process by which scholars from the root disciplines consider themselves to be members of the IR community, perhaps leaning towards economic, legal, historical or sociological perspectives but nonetheless of the community. It was during this time that scholars who self-identified as IR scholars saw for the first time their own intellectual offspring, their students, coming of age and being socialized into the norms and values of the community (examples included students of Coral Bell, Raymond Aron, Adda Bozeman and William Fox). A community needs this kind of reproduction to become sustainable.

Third, in some parts of the world, theoretical reflection became fashionable, and fashions eventually turned into recurring patterns of theoretical thought. The theoretical turn was the outcome of many micro-practices, and it would be misleading to identify a specific moment. However, among the significant events, was the Rockefeller-sponsored conference in 1954, even if its outcome was not what the organizers had hoped. In other words, realism did not become the dominant theoretical paradigm (except perhaps in the US and in textbooks). The outcome of five years of theorizing endeavours came with the volume edited by Fox (1959). Other Rockefeller Foundation-sponsored activities included the work of the British Committee on the Theory of International Politics, which resulted in *Diplomatic Investigations* (Butterfield and Wight, 1966; see also Dunne, 1998), and an initiative led by Raymond Aron in France to publish a journal special issue on political theory. In addition to these institution-sponsored activities, numerous individual scholars contributed to the theoretical turn (Waltz, 1959; Hoffmann, 1960; Aron, 1966). In the context of transnational community building, fellowship programmes enabled the exchange of ideas, and new books on the market were during this period reviewed on both sides of the Atlantic.

Theorizing became fashionable and a tool in processes of discipline formation in some but not all parts of the world. Instead of explicit theorizing, self-images focused on political and diplomatic practices. For instance, in newly independent states operational knowledge was more cherished or valued than abstract, specialized knowledge. This touches on the balance between science and applied science and its impact on the formation of scientific disciplines. Moreover, the uneven valuation of theory around the world was to lead four or five decades later to Acharya and Buzan's (2007) question, 'Why is there no non-western international relations theory?' The extended version of the question is 'Why is the scientific discipline of IR predominantly western, at least when it comes to theory building?'

Cold War II: 1970s and 1980s

The external environment of the IR community changed profoundly in the course of these two decades. Institutions of higher education experienced unprecedented growth. There was a mushrooming of new universities, which to some extent included an increase in the number of IR departments and programmes. Students arrived at university gates in huge numbers, and scholars were hired to teach them. The new recruits often brought with them new ideas about what IR was and ought to be. New ideas also floated in the public discourse, and even the US secretary of state, Henry Kissinger, talked about economic interdependence. In the community of IR scholars, the meaning of IR was contested (see Chapter 5). While some pleaded for its scope to be broadened to include IPE and transnational relations, others saw such widening as a threat to what they considered to be the core of the discipline and, thus, a *deroute* to be avoided (Kaiser, 1969; Strange, 1970; Waltz, 1979; Holsti, 1985; Yamamoto, 2011). However, the contending meanings of IR not only reflected the community's 'self' or internal differentiation, but they also played a role at the boundaries with other disciplinary communities. Had economists engaged in research on the linkages between International Politics and Economics, the rationale for the IR subdiscipline of IPE would have been less pronounced. But they did not. Had legal scholars engaged with the political and sociological dimensions of international institutions, the rationale for the IR subdiscipline of international organization would not be strong. But they did not. A third example of boundary formation was peace research: while one side would ask if peace researchers were part of 'our' IR community, peace researchers frequently asked if they wanted to be part of 'the' IR community. The fourth example concerns the inroads made during the 1970s throughout the western world by Marxist scholars (see e.g. Anderson, 1973), which prompted questions similar to those asked about peace research, for instance, whether world system theory was IR and, in turn, whether Wallerstein was part of the scholarly IR community.

As we have seen, Anthony Cohen deliberately downplays the role of structure (i.e. form and organization), focusing attention instead on symbols and meaning(s). He argues that structure does not determine behaviour and that meanings should not be derived from structure. In the present context, structures could be the universities in which IR scholars live major parts of their lives, and it can also be the professional associations in which they exchange ideas about their research. Following Cohen's approach, I will not analyse how such structures have an impact on the scholarly community, but it makes sense to analyse the interplay between structure on the one hand and symbols and meanings on the other.

By 1971 the ISA was ready to internationalize its activities, thereby transcending national boundaries and, thus, in a sense, returning to the transnationalism of the interwar years. To prepare the move, a policy-making meeting was held in Ohio, followed by a meeting at Rockefeller's Villa Bellagio in Italy (Teune, 1982). The IR community had been consolidated as almost 2,000 of its members joined the ISA, and these members were more confident than the 60 who had paid their membership fees in 1963. For some members, the move to internationalize activities and membership had a downside, not least that the early ISA ideology of organizing scholar-practitioner conferences had to be abandoned. 'We' in the community would no longer be those who organize such conferences: this implied that there was now a boundary in the previously close relationship between scholar and practitioner. That characterized most organizations for much of the 20th century. We should not generalize too much in this context. Moon and Kim (2002) point out in relation to South Korea, 'Most of those who have served as the president of KAIS [Korean Association of International Studies] have been recruited as ministers, ambassadors, and national assembly men' (p. 46). In South Korea IR scholars were called to fulfil functions outside academia, which showed that their broad competences were valued by society and state. The move by the ISA to internationalize membership stood in stark contrast to other important national international studies associations (e.g. KAIS, Japan Association of International Relations (JAIR) and the Nordic Committee, the latter being one of the few regional organizations and thus, in a sense, a transnational enterprise). Indeed, even more importantly, numerous parts of the world did not yet have professional associations in the field, reflecting the poor organization of the community and the relatively poor formalization of its values, norms and standards.

But this state of affairs was about to change. One example was the UK, where the BCCIS morphed into the BISA. A second example was the Nordic Committee, which had for some time relied on external subsidies from the Nordic Council. When political commitments and financial flows dried up, the committee had to reinvent itself and became the Nordic International Studies Association (NISA). What in the present context is significant is that these organizational changes reflected the changes in the values and meanings among the members of the IR community. The BISA case illustrated a general change in community values. BISA should not only be for that which Susan Strange (1995: 289) called 'the barons', the network of the 'old boys' who had not only initiated but had also controlled the British IR community for so long. Conferences should be for individual members of the association, not for delegates who had been cherry-picked by the barons. Conference panels should complement plenary meetings, thereby opening the gates to greater access, engagement and exchange. Decisions about publications should not entirely be determined by 'old fox' gate-keeping editors, but rather informed by recommendations of anonymous peer reviewers. This was a general trend in the trade, although the speed of change varied significantly across countries and regions.

When JAIR, KAIS and BISA received company from an increasing number of national and regional associations, the policy of internationalizing the ISA by means of individual memberships entered dire straits. While some IR scholars from outside the US joined the ISA (and were strongly encouraged to do so), most did not. As Teune (1982) observes, 'Those were difficult years because of the growing estrangement of European scholars from their U.S. colleagues' (p. 4). Instead, they created their own associations. By the end of the 1980s, approximately a dozen associations had been created worldwide, and the ISA had to add a component to its individual membership scheme: partner associations. This innovative scheme consolidated the community of scholars, who now networked and exchanged ideas more than ever. At the same time, the relationship between ISA and other international studies associations was hotly contested for a while, not least because of the ISA's (short-lived) idea that partner associations had a duty to report their activities to the self-styled ISA mothership. The network was also biased in that the ISA cultivated relations with its partners while the latter seldom showed much interest in cultivating relations with each other.

In summary, the 1970s and 1980s was a period during which the values cherished by the community completely changed. It was a kind of cultural revolution and one that had a profound impact on the discipline.

The IR community in a globalizing world

With the end of the Cold War, the Soviet Union and the east–west division of Europe and most of the world, the IR community began reconsidering its values, its self-image and the boundaries both within itself and with other disciplinary communities. The external framework conditions that had had a significant impact on the community during the 40 formative Cold War years were in the process of being transformed into something else – what US president George Bush called 'that vision thing'.

However, in a comprehensive analysis the dramatic changes in the external environment were only one among several factors. The quantitative growth of the discipline happened at a time when IR as a narrowly defined social science experienced serious problems. The behavioural revolution, for instance, ran out of steam; positivism proved unable to deliver on its promises; and processes of globalization made the ring-fencing of national politics unviable. At this time national IR communities also began to (re)discover each other, occasionally producing cultural encounters of difference.

As we saw in Chapter 3, it was time to take stock of the discipline and to point in new directions. Given that what we do is intimately linked to who or what we are, it is hardly surprising that the IR community members began by reconsidering their identity, that is, the 'self' of the community, the other(s) and the boundaries between self and other. Steve Smith's (1995) chapter 'Ten self-images of a discipline' nailed a widespread feeling at the time: that 'image' in the singular had been replaced by 'images' in the plural. In conventional style, Smith used theory to define the discipline rather than subject matter, the questions asked or the sociology of the IR community. The nature of scientific disciplines received limited attention, indeed hardly any attention at all. It would not be far-fetched to hypothesize that each of the ten self-images was cultivated by its own distinct grouping with the community. The examples in this section aim at illustrating some of the general ways in which the IR community (or parts thereof) constructed meaning by means of symbols and values.

During the last 30 years, the IR community membership is estimated to have reached more than 20,000 members.[6] The community sustains a discipline supporting at least a dozen subdisciplines, more than a handful of theoretical traditions and a subject matter that is as broad as it gets. Hence, it is not difficult to understand why internal differentiation or fragmentation characterizes the community. However, it is also easy to observe that members, despite the internal differentiation, consistently choose to attend specialized IR conferences, to publish in and edit specialized IR journals, and to run teaching programmes at all levels, including PhD programmes aimed at socializing future members into the community and serving societies and states with specialized knowledge to enable them to manage foreign relations. In short, some members may not always acknowledge their membership of the community but nonetheless they act as though they are members. Even members who prefer IR as an interdisciplinary enterprise shy away from attending conferences about biology, linguistics or whatever disciplines they want to bring together to better understand a given case, region or event.

The so-called third debate – positivism versus postpositivism – is essentially a package of encounters between the various quarters of the community, and therefore a debate that mirrors contending values and norms, for which reason it will not come to an end any time soon. One segment of the community self-identifies as dissident, which symbolically expresses the growing estrangement of scholars who do not identify with the discipline; for this reason they are happy to observe and in some cases even promote and legitimize the fragmentation of the community. In opposing a designated (or imagined) mainstream, they see themselves at the boundary and engage in fringe research interests. They contest IR but tend to embrace 'international thought'; their subject matter is not international relations but 'the international'; and they replace discipline with a libertarian or laissez-faire approach. In the case of poststructuralism they are equipped with a licence to deconstruct. A second segment observes the paradox that the IR community tends to reflect national boundaries and is therefore a not so international community. While most professional associations are identified by and function within national boundaries, some take pride in being transnational, thereby actively addressing the paradox. NISA, EISA, the Central and Eastern European International Studies Association and WISC, for example, are in contrast to the ISA and its dual identity of organizing a transnational (in fact global) membership while taking pride in being a North American or US ISA.[7]

Despite their behaviours, values and attitudes, some community members do not feel they belong to a community. This is understandable. After all, community members are often dispersed or in minority situations in their everyday practices within departments or faculties. They may also prefer IR to be not a discipline but rather an interdisciplinary site. Instead of a discipline, they see a field of study. They see individuals instead of a community, even if they do not subscribe to Margaret Thatcher's dictum 'There is no such thing as society'.

Given the considerable variation in self-image, there is also predictable variation in terms of images of other communities. Since the early 1990s, the notion of hegemony has been attached to several others, not least the American IR community (Kahler, 1993; Crawford and Jarvis, 2001; Smith, 2002). Occasionally, the other is not the IR community in the US but broadly the community in 'the west'. The problem with hegemony classic is that empirical evidence often points in other directions. Using meticulous empirical research, Louise Turton (2015) shows how hegemony is more imagined than real. In turn, one can think about the functions such hegemony imaginations might have (Jørgensen et al, 2017) as well as the opportunities that emerge after hegemony (Jørgensen, 2014).

In the designation of others, 'parochial' is a second keyword. And in the context of an IR community that takes prides in its international mind or outlook, parochialism, like hegemony, does not have positive connotations. Perhaps the most widespread result of a parochial approach is that others are totally out of sight or are deemed irrelevant. A competing practice is to think that my world is *the* world. This is what Chris Brown (2001) hints at with the chapter title 'Fog in the Channel: Continental relations theory isolated'. When an author conducts research for a state-of-the-art article and 97 per cent of the contributions are from his own country, some parochialism might be at play. Critics of western IR scholarship expand this to the global level, arguing that western scholars tend to write about disciplinary affairs as if it were *their* discipline. As we shall discuss in Chapter 7, they may have a point, but the problem is that it typically also applies to their own studies.

Communities cultivating other disciplines are frequently seen as others. Political Science is a frequent other. It is sometimes seen as a prison within which IR is malfunctioning (Rosenberg, 2016), and sometimes as an imperialist discipline attempting to suppress IR (Manning, 1954, 1957a; 1962a). Historians have been seen as extremely negative towards IR, and economists are seen as the force behind rationalism.

Divisions within the IR community are widespread and give rise to a colourful image of the discipline. If isms are considered evil (Lake, 2011), it presumably follows that the segment within the community that represents or cherishes the isms is seen as different from the spotter of evil. Whereas being an appointed part of the mainstream is typically not a self-image but a useful label in processes of othering, being critical is very much a self-image. In this perspective, others are sometimes in need of help or emancipation, such as the silenced or unheard global voices, while still others are in need of citations. In the latter case some editors can help. For instance in the submission guidelines of *International Studies Review* the editors highlight the following (actually three times), 'Much recent research shows a gender citation gap in international relations scholarship (Maliniak et al, 2013; Mitchell et al, 2013). We encourage authors to think about these patterns as they finalize their manuscripts.'[8] A second example of contemporary norms guiding professional behaviour is demonstrated in the Sharoni versus Lebow case, which also illustrates the stance of a major professional association.[9]

The boundaries between self-image and images of others are very dynamic, meaning that the configuration of fault-lines is bound to change across time and place, occasionally triggering tectonic shifts. Whereas the bashing of idealism had its heyday in the 1950s, the collective stabbing of neorealism is a 1990s vintage. Paradoxically, just as social constructivism produced one of its finest products (Wendt, 1999), was 'recognized' by mainstream scholars (Katzenstein et al, 1998) and was validated as an empirical research programme (Finnemore and Sikkink, 2001), interest in social constructivism somehow faded and was eventually complemented by a number of new enterprises, some small and others considerably larger – eclecticism, new materialism, practice theory (Bueger and Gadinger, 2014), micro-studies, critical and postcritical, global IR, decentring.

Conclusion

It is within communities that things happen, that community members play various roles, represent and stand up for various values, and cultivate various life forms. The IR community is no exception. It is the community that develops scholarly standards, (changing) patterns of discourse as well as diverse scholarly horizons. Against this background, it is nothing less than a mystery that disciplinary studies tend to pay so little attention to features of community. This chapter aims at countering the neglect and therefore highlights the significance of the scholarly community that cultivates the discipline, including its values, norms and ways of thinking. Given that the community varies over time, the chapter is structured along temporal lines. The chapter underlines the challenge facing contemporary scholars to appraise former scholarly practices, as such and as representing values and norms that were prevalent in former times. The chapter demonstrates how contemporary scholars at all times have tended to dismiss selected former practices while at the same time polishing appreciative self-images. The challenge we face is thus to board the time machine, travel to some point in the future, not to explore where we will be at that point but to look back retrospectively at early 21st-century practices, and to decide which values and norms should be dismissed and which praised.

7

Globalizing International Relations?

Introduction

It is intriguing, almost amusing, to watch how the disciplinary *terroiriste* have entered the discipline of International Relations in the last few decades, sometimes called just IR, presumably to avoid too much discipline.[1] *Terroir* and *denominazione origine* are no longer a *domaine réservé* for wine, cheese or foie gras. For the IR *terroiriste* it matters, and for some matters beyond imagination, in which garden a given theory has grown and which gardener cultivated it. In short, origin matters and, it seems to me, the issue should therefore be part of disciplinary meta-studies. My previous engagements in this distinct field of study have taught me that the relatively small *terroiriste* community is deeply split, and the label may actually be all that is holding the community together. Given this state of affairs, it is with a mix of reluctance and persistence that I address the impact of *terroir*, including designations of local and global.

During the last two decades, there have been ever more vocal calls to make the discipline more 'international' or 'global'. This trend builds on the curious idea that IR is a *spécialité américaine* (Grosser, 1956) or 'an American social science' (Hoffman, 1977). Some suggest that IR is under 'Anglo-American hegemony' (Holsti, 1985) or, more vaguely, 'a not so international discipline' (Wæver, 1998).[2] Other observers claim that IR is a Eurocentric or western discipline (Hobson, 2012). In a similar vein, Martin Griffiths and Terry O'Callaghan (2001) think that 'the idea of a discipline of IR is little more than a thinly disguised parochialism masquerading as a global field of study' (p. 188), a perspective seemingly shared by Chris Brown (2001), who states that 'the very idea that one actually needs a discipline of IR may be tied up with a particular worldview' (p. 218). It is worth noting that the various calls share more than the idea of a more international discipline; they also share a western origin.

In any case, counter-arguments followed. With reference to the Anglo-American hegemony, some were eager to point to pronounced differences between American and British perspectives (Smith, 1985), instead emphasizing American hegemony and thus taking British IR off the hook (Smith, 1996; 2002). Others point to contributions from Continental Europe (Jørgensen, 2000; Groom and Mandaville, 2001). In this context, Groom and Mandaville (2001) ask in upbeat fashion: 'What hegemony? ... There is now a nascent "European IR community" that is alive and well and living, for the most part, in the EU ... There are ... no hegemonies, something that may also be true beyond the confines of the EU and North America' (p. 163).[3] The last part of the sentence is particularly important, because *if* it is 'true beyond the confines of the EU and North America', then what, if anything, ought to be done? If it is not true, there may be a problem and problems call for solutions.

As well as examining the impact of *terroir*, the chapter aim to outline a prudent course between the Scylla of local and the Charybdis of global in the hope that such a middle course will produce positive outcomes of some of the current endeavours to further globalize the discipline. In this context, the chapter suggests that we should take 'global' literally and thus practise the preached message, that is, conduct an exercise in genuine inclusion, which in turn implies that the process of globalizing the discipline cannot begin with burning 'degenerate' books or erasing IR with a western origin. Finally, I should highlight that, while the preceding chapters outline answers to the question 'What is International Relations?', they also address the issue of the 'global', thereby contributing to demonstrating that the discipline *is* indeed global, *is* diverse, in terms of practice. The main difference between the previous chapters and this one is that this addresses the issue explicitly.

It seems to me that two mega-trends characterize contemporary IR scholarship on the issue of globalizing the discipline: the local innocence and the globalizing telos-free trends. I briefly highlight the key features of each and summarize the sizeable literatures produced by scholars within each trend. I also point out the main inconsistences and limitations of each trend. Finally, I suggest a pragmatic way forward that continues to promise a discipline that is global in both approach and coverage.

What is local?

The antonym to global is local. So to understand what global is, it is useful to begin with an explication of local. There is a recurrent pattern in IR discourse whereby authors seldom employ 'local' with positive connotations. 'Local' tends to connote parochial, someone who has a challenged global outlook or worse. For IR scholars, it is quite understandably not a widespread self-image, frequently appearing instead as one of the main characteristics attached to stigmatizing practices of other scholars. This book takes the opposite view. Local is not to be avoided but is simply a condition for scholarly practices; it contributes to the diversity of the discipline and provides a key rationale for what we do, that is, produce scientific knowledge about how various actors negotiate local-global relations. In short, we should not automatically admonish but actually cherish the local, while acknowledging that there are also problems in this solution.

I begin by emphasizing that the environment in which we are situated influences what we decide to observe, as well as our actual observations, to some degree at least and in ways we are not always conscious of.[4] Our individual and institutional Archimedean points prompt us to determine what and where 'international' is.[5] In this context the concept of *Standortgebundenheit*, coined by the sociologist Karl Mannheim and brought into IR by Hans Morgenthau (1962) to explain the different roles theory might play, becomes highly relevant.[6] Other scholars share Mannheim's perspective, including the historian Fernand Braudel (1972), who reflects on the significance of nine years of residence in Algeria on his scholarship: 'I believe that this spectacle, the Mediterranean seen from the opposite side, upside down, had considerable impact on my vision of history' (p. 450). Dozens of central European IR scholars fled Nazi Germany, taking their local experiences and outlooks with them, and it became their fate and challenge to make sense of these experiences and outlooks in environments that were significantly different from those they were forced to leave behind. When John Herz migrated to the US, for instance, he crossed the Atlantic with '200 years of European intellectual history' in his luggage and became 'a traveller between all worlds' (Puglierin, 2008; see also Hacke and Puglierin, 2007; Reichwein and Rösch, 2021). In the present context, the specificities of Morgenthau, Mannheim, Braudel and Herz do not matter. What matters is that each in their own way illustrates how local is a condition that should not be denigrated. Actually, the local is, even with its many limitations, often to be preferred to a bland globality without qualities.

'Local' occasionally appears ethnocentric, but rarely in an appreciative fashion. Audrey Alejandro (2017b; 2018; see also Jørgensen et al, 2017) is an exception. Drawing on anthropological literature, she observes how the specialized literature on ethnocentrism, 'has effectively detached itself from focusing only on the discriminatory side of ethnocentrism' (Alejandro, 2017b: 17).[7] She points out how ethnocentrism functions as one of the important tools employed by communities around the world to boost their resilience and, as a side effect, to help constitute diversity. Thus armed, she offers the punchline that 'the question is not to suppress ethnocentrism, but rather to adjust perceptions towards the in-groups and the out-groups in order to balance the level of influence and exchange between different groups' (Alejandro, 2017b: 18; 2017c). She concludes that 'the purpose of reflexivity is not to address *others'* problems; it is to break the vicious circle of criticism in order directly to face the effects that we ourselves produce through our own socialisation' (Alejandro, 2017b: 20, emphasis original; see also Bilgin, 2017; Alejandro, 2017c).

Alejandro's argument is very important, not least because it prompts one to reconsider the meaning of key concepts thoroughly, to rethink causal flows in both empirical research and normative reasoning, as well as to see more clearly and more detached from conventional critical wisdom how the essentially contested concepts that I use to structure the book are connected. 'Local', 'parochial' and 'ethnocentric' thus may share some features but otherwise have completely different meanings. While it may be an uncomfortable fact for some, Eurocentrism is not necessarily the root cause of all evils (Žižek, 1998; see also Kapur, 2018). Practices of theorizing are shaped by their embeddedness in cultural forms; diversity is among the spill-overs from the condition of being local; and the IR community is full of ethnocentric attitudes towards both in-groups and out-groups. In many cases, community resilience is apparently much needed and ethnocentrism is therefore boosted.

To avoid potential misunderstanding, I would like to emphasize that the cherishing of local is not a blank cheque to accept that anything local goes. In a chapter titled 'Fog in the Channel: Continental relations theory isolated', Chris Brown (2001) hints at certain local British perspectives on Europe and the world (15 years before Brexit). He uses the image to effectively address issues of diversity and parochialism in the discipline. Indeed, it is a universal predicament. Many IR scholars do not care about geo-epistemological issues and believe that they just do IR. They apply available theories in more or less comprehensive research projects. Often, they do not engage with scholarship beyond their own national boundaries. Nonetheless, or rather as a result of this restriction, they strongly believe in the universal applicability of the discipline's theories and methodologies. Studies may trigger conceptual refinement, such as Walt's (1987) studies of the Middle East, from balance of power to balance of threats, yet without questioning the key features of realism or the discipline. Critics are critical of what they perceive to be 'the discipline', and especially the part of the IR community that produces mainstream scholarship with local, Eurocentric and parochial characteristics. In this fashion, they offer a diagnosis of

Table 7.1: Unpacking concepts and enabling novel ways of identifying problems and solutions (fill in the blanks)

		Scope	
		Particular	Universal
Space	Local		
	Global		

an illness and, on that basis, hand out a prescription emphasizing the importance of making the discipline more international or more global (see Table 7.1). The discipline should be decentred, decolonized – de-*something*. We end up with a dense fabric of normative, ought-to-be, ought-to-do statements and a lightly knit canvas of studies about how the discipline really is (for exceptions see Ford Foundation, 1976; Czempiel, 1986; Hellmann et al, 2003).

With reference to strategies for globalizing the discipline, some scholars explore the promises of so-called homegrown theorizing (Aydinli and Mathews, 2000; Aydinli and Biltekin, 2018; Kuru, 2018). Notably the strategy concerns not the discipline per se but theorizing within the discipline. According to Aydinli and Biltekin (2018), homegrown theorizing is 'original theorizing in the periphery about the periphery' (p. 45). They draw a distinction between three forms of this: referential homegrown theorizing, homegrown alterations and authentic homegrown theories. While the first concerns IR theorizing that relies on non-IR local thought and the export of concepts into IR, 'homegrown alterations' are about reconstructing western ideas to match local contexts. Finally, authentic homegrown IR theories are built on the basis of original concepts that designate peripheral experiences. The strategy has promise, not least because it goes beyond the critique of theorizing in the designated core, but it unnecessarily reduces the scope to theorizing about the periphery, as if theorists in the periphery are unable to theorize at the systemic level or about the designated core. For instance, Samir Amin's theory of Eurocentrism would not qualify as homegrown, and the same applies to theorizing in China about international order.

IR going 'global'?

The second trend, globalizing IR, perhaps began with the claim that IR is 'a not so international discipline' (Wæver, 1998) and continues with ever more calls to globalize IR. Occasionally, scholars phrase this in terms of a normative emancipation project: let us emancipate the non-western world from the yoke of western knowledge, the latter characterized as Eurocentric, colonial or worse. The suggested strategies to depart from or to abandon existing knowledge include, for instance, 'provincializing IR', 'decentring IR' and 'decolonizing

IR' (Shani, 2007; Sabaratnam, 2011; Taylor, 2012; Vasilaki, 2012; Nayak and Selbin, 2013; Shih and Hwang, 2018).

The notion of decentring, which has been widely employed, refers to an interest in making a seemingly hierarchical world a more flat one, that is, changing the uneven distribution of abstract knowledge production. If we agree that there is 'one world, many perspectives' and not 'many worlds, many perspectives', we at least share a point of departure for our journey into interpretations, representations, understandings and explanations of what 'globalizing the discipline' might mean. While decentring sounds nice and innocent, the risk is that successful decentring may equal a number of isolated islands of discipline, each cultivating its own concepts and theories, norms for good scholarship and adequate procedures for rigorous scientific analysis. If the shared key concepts disappear – because the (imagined) hegemon has disappeared – we could end up having a limited or no shared language. Decentring thus entaild risks, especially the risk caused by the absence of the common goods the imagined (benign) hegemon, operating in universal terms, provide. Without a core body of literature, theory and key concepts, the risk clearly is that communication will be hampered. This is Holsti's (1985) concern elevated to the global level (see Chapter 5).

Moreover, globalizers tend to have concerns about the applicability of 'western' concepts. How can western concepts be relevant for research on the non-western world? In this fashion, globalizers share the axiom of the non-transferability of western concepts and ideas with the current among Arab intellectuals that Sadiq Jalal al-Azm (1981; see also Achcar, 2008) labels 'Islamanic'. Islamanic intellectuals and scholars have protested the use of western concepts in studies of the Arab world. According to al-Azm, they thereby practised a kind of reverse orientalism. Russophiles also tend to subscribe to the non-applicability axiom (Tsygankov, 2008), and a similar rationale informed the desperate search among some Chinese scholars for an IR with Chinese characteristics (Callahan, 2001; Song, 2001). The outright rejection of the transferability of concepts and ideas inevitably leads to 1,000 isolated islands, each characterized by its own body of knowledge; notably, knowledge that is incomprehensible and theories that are inapplicable beyond their boundaries. Instead of going beyond a not so international discipline, we could end up with an even less international or global discipline.

Paradoxically, IR is occasionally seen as a Eurocentric discipline.[8] The primary reason IR is sometimes called Eurocentric is that European conceptions of statehood define the units of the international system, and 19th-century European power politics have been used as a template for realist images of international politics. Moreover, many key IR concepts have their origins in the European state system and European diplomacy, such as sovereignty, international law and alliances. Finally, some IR theories or theoretical traditions can also be traced to European origins: liberalism, realism, the English School and so on. Notably, all these characteristics apply to old Europe but not contemporary Europe.[9] In most IR textbooks, the EU is more or less absent, perhaps with the exception of a brief introduction to the EU as an international organization. Hence, fertilizing IR theories with insights from contemporary Europe remains a major task, not something to avoid. Unfortunately, such theoretical innovation is unlikely to come out of Europe, especially because IR scholars in Europe tend to focus on 'domestic' European 'international' affairs – in this manner, they are Eurocentric.[10]

However, counter-evidence regarding the European origins of concepts can also be identified, and the list of this evidence is in fact rather long. Though there are exceptions, European IR scholars have not been leading in theory building for a long time. Major contemporary theoretical perspectives – rational choice, social constructivism, principal agent models, game theory and discourse theory – do not have particularly strong European characteristics. European IR scholars do not enjoy the volume of the US–American single market, and the European IR community is too diverse and dispersed to have a significant impact on global disciplinary trajectories. While the European state system in the 19th century constitutes a template for some scholars, many scholars around the world find it irrelevant. Finally, IR is a discipline in which major theoretical traditions hardly pay attention to the EU as an international actor. IR textbooks routinely describe a state-centric world in which the EU does not feature as constituting in terms of constituting a system unit, and therefore also drops out of standard, country-focused statistics.

In short, charges of Eurocentrism seem to be largely unfounded and old hat. The aspirations of processes aimed at decentring or globalizing the discipline tend to be contested. For some, the endeavour is to create new universals (Lizée, 2011). Others seek specific languages and thus non-universals. Still others seek new universals, yet are strangely cleansed for universals with a western origin. It is pitched as elite versus elite. No matter the distinct preferences in this contest, the notion of universalism merits serious attention. The notion of universalism does not figure prominently in the earlier account of the globalizing IR literature. By contrast, as we saw, Chris Brown (2001) believes that the feature is significant and that the discipline has strong cosmopolitan characteristics. In this way, Brown reduces the discipline to a product of the American garden and claims that a precondition for globalizing IR is to dismantle it. While I reject both the premise of the argument and the derived prescription, the universalism issue holds promise, and we shall return to it in the last section.

In conclusion, while the globalizing trend attracts the mind with a broad range of vaguely stated promises, it reminds me foremost of the old European maps of the world, characterized as they were by significant blank spots, reflecting the parts of the world left blank and declared undiscovered. The globalizing literature is in many ways an internal western critique, a form of navel gazing, not least because critics largely neglect the actually existing scholarship of their undiscovered world. They show limited interest in homemade theorizing, neglect for instance Japanese IR traditions and conveniently overlook the disastrous *dependencia* literature. They show no appreciation for Taiwanese applications of game theory and seemingly find IR with Chinese characteristics sufficiently different from appropriate templates for globalizing IR. Similarly, they conveniently overlook the uncomfortable fact that most of those planned to be emancipated tend to prefer theoretical orientations that the critics abandoned decades ago. Indicators in support of the claim put forward in the previous sentence include TRIP survey data, according to which the postpositivist turn has not arrived in east Asia and that almost twice as many scholars not in the west subscribe to realism as in the west, indeed it appears that in some countries more than one third of all scholars identify with realism as their paradigm (Wemheuer-Vogelaar et al, 2016; see also Tickner and Wæver 2009: 334–5[11]). Moreover, it is remarkable that Wiebke Wemheuer-Vogelaar et al suggest that, 'at just 6.27%, Marxism in IR is arguably on life support around the world' (2016: 27). They do not comment on the state of IR feminism, which at less than 2 per cent, has even fewer followers.

Seven passages: beyond Eurocentrism and decentrism

If neither centric nor decentric approaches promise passages to the global, then what does? This section follows up on the no hegemonies claim and focuses on the situation after hegemony, that is, after the imagined hegemonies.[12] The following seven passages to the global seem particularly promising.

The first passage is not about concepts, theories or journal metrics; it is organizational. Acknowledging the failure of IPSA to make IR more than a marginal sideshow within the study of politics, and instead of accepting the ISA as a US-managed quasi-global mothership association, WISC was founded in 1993 (Buzan, nd). The objective was exceptionally pragmatic and low-key, for instance aiming at the coordination of conference calendars around the world. One decade later, WISC launched the tradition of organizing triennial conferences, to some degree modelled on a multiple-ISAs organized conference in Hong Kong in 2001.[13] However, the first four WISC conferences took place in Europe, the first in Istanbul in 2005, followed by Ljubljana (2008), Porto (2011) and Frankfurt (2014). These conferences demonstrated an increasing awareness of the 'global' inclusion problem and yet, for many known and unknown reasons, limited the inclusion of scholars from beyond the west. The fifth conference took place in Taiwan (2017) and was much more inclusive of scholars based in Asia. The planned conference in Buenos Aires (2020) would have included more scholars based in Latin America, but with its postponement to 2022 as result of the COVID-19 pandemic, we do not know the final configuration of attendees. Given that WISC conferences are triennial, the ISA convention remains the biggest and most inclusive annual global hub. Nonetheless, it is also the pet target of the globalizers, who are always eager to engage in west-centric critique. These globalizers, however, demonstrate limited interest in attending conventions organized by, for instance, the Mexican, Chinese or Russian associations. This is a pity, because passages to the global should be genuinely global. In addition to organizing conventional conferences, professional associations could join forces and organize 100 tailor-made workshops devoted to theorists building suitable theories for the 21st century (see also Jørgensen, 2018).

The second passage begins by acknowledging that the post-western discussion does not point in any distinct or specific direction, except that there may be no direction home (Ikeda 2010; Shahi & Ascione, 2016). In other words, the option of recreating IR in the image of an imaginary golden past is not an option, or at least it should not be an option. At the same time, it should be remembered that IR scholars generally pay limited attention to the post-western IR discussion and tend to soldier on along well-established avenues. This may be our good fortune, simply because major parts of the contributions to the post-western IR discussion tend to be more ideological than analytical, richer in opinions than data and, paradoxically, more western than any other label of geographical origin. If, despite these limits, the post-western IR discussion can enrich our discipline, it can be seen as a passage.

The third passage concerns the promotion of non-western theoretical perspectives on civilizational and imperial global orders. Such a promotion would go beyond state-centric biases but is not without problems. The employment of distinctly non-western concepts is obviously a notable challenge to lazy western minds and a highly disquieting factor in the (de)construction of 'our' western world-views. Yet it is an even greater cognitive challenge to acknowledge that non-western theoretical reflections tend to be primed by features that critical IR aims at problematizing. The following three challenges for a sound global IR discipline therefore amount to a mission nearly impossible.

In the first place, it is not particularly exceptional to think in terms of exceptionalism. Scholarship on Eurocentrism, orientalism and European integration documents, despite notable differences and sometimes unintentionally, how Europeans in practice and theory are no strangers to thinking in terms of exceptionalism. However, it is well known that American exceptionalism is also a phenomenon of considerable consequence (Ruggie, 2004).

Likewise, scholarship on Russia, India and China demonstrates the existence and significance of exceptionalism with Russian, Indian and Chinese characteristics. Analysts report and/or represent conceptions of unique and/or primordial Russian, Indian and Chinese (state) civilizations (Pye, 1992; Tsygankov, 2008; Ollapally and Rajagopalan, 2012; Chacko, 2013; Dugin, 2014a). Indeed, exceptionalist thinking seems predominant around the world, which makes it somewhat difficult to find exceptions to this seemingly universal way of thinking.

Nor is it particularly exceptional to think in terms of ethnocentrism. In the Russian case, ethnocentrism is among the key characteristics of the neo-Eurasianist conception of global order, with notions of Russian cultural superiority accompanied by prescriptions of power maximization and territorial advances. Perpetually torn between western and eastern civilizations, Russia must apparently choose. Yet neo-Eurasianists reject the dilemma by claiming a distinct Russian civilizational status, thus using in-betweenness as a source of identity. In Global South perspectives, partly outside and partly inside the IR discipline, cultural or moral superiority claims are ubiquitous and cherished. As a leading Muslim Brotherhood social theorist, Sayyid Qutb (2006); see also Khatab, 2006) claims a moral superiority based on Islamic faith. While Qutb was not an IR scholar, his claim finds resonance in the Islamic world (on IR and Islam, see Tadjbakhsh, 2010; Abdelkader et al, 2016). Confucianism is characterized by a significant degree of ethnocentrism, specifically Han Chinese ethnocentrism. This version of ethnocentrism comes as a full package, including ideas about non-Han races being barbarians. In India, there is a widespread idea that the Indian state civilization is more peaceful than most and obviously morally superior (Chacko, 2013).

Finally, it is not particularly European or western to cultivate universal ideas. Like western liberalism, Confucianism is universalistic (see notions like *tianxia* and expectations about a global order with Chinese characteristics), beginning with China's peaceful rise. Yet contending universal ideologies are bound to cause diplomatic challenges. It is hardly surprising that China–EU relations are characterized by 'conceptual gaps' (Pan, 2012), that is, concepts that are shared globally but with contending meanings or key terms that are known or have meaning only in some parts of the world. In Chinese nationalist discourse, the notion of 'a century of humiliation' is routinely cultivated, whereas a European version, such as 'a century of decline', hardly exists in nationalist discourse. Likewise, important concepts that Europeans take for granted, such as the Renaissance or the Enlightenment, may understandably provoke cognitive turbulence elsewhere.

In a genuinely global IR discipline, it will be difficult to acknowledge that Europe (or the west) does not enjoy a monopoly of exceptionalism, ethnocentrism and universalism, for which reason criticism of Eurocentrism increasingly appears to represent a critique of yesterday's state of affairs. However, the mega-trend of Europe's relative decline and the related global power shifts make critique of a centric perspective more relevant than ever, so why not make it a universal critique of centric perspectives of all sorts?

The fourth passage concerns one of the key issues when imagining a global discipline. In concrete terms, it requires a thorough examination of what 'universal' and 'particular' refer to. In Pierre Lizée's (2011) terms, 'Engaging all these questions, though, means a step forward for the discipline, one that entails a re-examination of its basic language about what is universal and what is particular in international affairs. This is the last element in the reinvention of international studies proposed in this book' (p. 13). Lizée (2011) continues with how

> the key authors and texts which have shaped the nature and evolution of international studies as a discipline must be brought in when we consider these issues. To do otherwise would leave unresolved the one issue which must be addressed by international studies at the moment: the core canon of the discipline would remain unchanged, the 'rise of the rest' would proceed apace, and the gap between the discipline and the world it now has to explain would grow, without ever being bridged. This is where, in the end, the most crucial challenge for international studies could lie at this time. (p. 13)

The fifth passage concerns the dialectics between general and specific studies, in other words, the relationship between IR and regional studies (area studies). I will use Middle East Studies to illustrate my point. It seems to me that, instead of continuing in the orthodox track of critique of orientalism, focusing on western representations of the Middle East, Middle East Studies could focus on the straightforward task of contributing to our understanding of how the Middle East really is, and, in turn, point to cases where critique of orientalism got it either right or wrong. Similarly, it could also point to instances of orientalist prejudices within what we could call the wider Middle East, such as Ottoman orientalism (Makdisi, 2002; Eldem, 2010; on Ottoman identity, see Ergul, 2012) or Egyptian research on Persia (Hammad, 2015). Such a move would raise awareness of representations not only in the west but globally. Moreover, instead of continuing in the track of critiquing Eurocentrism, Middle East Studies could focus on distinctions between genuine Eurocentrism and ideology-informed critiques, such as how critiques of Eurocentrism in the Middle East tend to morph into occidentalism or to merge with the widespread anti-Europeanism that underpins much political action (see Mohamed 2015).[14] Moreover, the post-western IR discussion could be used to encourage theorizing among IR scholars in the Middle East, thus crystallizing knowledge in theoretical form about the Middle East and the global environment in which it is situated. IR scholars situated in the Middle East could critically reconstruct IR theoretical traditions in the Middle East, including their origins, trajectories and potential futures. In other words, the post-western IR discussion could be used to encourage engagement in critical self-reflection on paths chosen, rightly or wrongly, to encourage reflections on future directions and priorities. Such activities may not apply to Middle East Studies more broadly, but they would give Middle East Studies scholars across the world a different kind of partner in the Middle East.[15]

The sixth passage concerns non-western IR theory in which key terms tend to include 'empire' and 'civilization'. The primary problem is that each term is characterized by limited conceptualization. While relations between civilizations and the state system are not addressed in any systematic fashion, intriguing suggestions have flourished. Moreover, empire and civilization are both critiqued and normatively promoted. While critique of western imperialism is to be expected, the promotion of non-western empires might be slightly surprising. Ahmet Davutoglu, the author of the preface to *Civilizations and World Order* (Dallmayr et al, 2014), is both a former Turkish prime minister and an IR professor, the author of *Strategic Depth* (2005), a blueprint for 'neo-Ottomanism', which is a highly contested term in Turkish identity politics (Taspinar, 2008; see also Davutoglu, 1994; see also Murinson, 2006). In Iranian identity politics, identity formation processes draw on not only Islamic sources but also imperial and civilizational sources. In the China case, the idea of a harmonious world has striking similarities with imperial peace.

In Russia, Alexander Dugin and other neo-Eurasianists do not hide their appetite for a new Russian empire, specifically a (re)integrated Soviet empire without communism.[16] The colourful world of Dugin's world-views is less interesting for present purposes than that he represents wider sentiments in Russia. Thus, Andrei Tsygankov (2008) introduces the rich tradition of civilizational debates in Russia and situates the civilizational perspectives along two axes: their identity – Europe/the west versus the non-west – and their degree of essentialism. In Russian civilizational debates, it is particularly the Eurasianist current of thinking that cultivates counter-hegemonic (but not anti-hegemonic) perspectives. Whereas balance-of-power theory provides a rationale for avoiding hegemony, Eurasianists seek to counter and replace what they see as an existing western hegemony. Drawing on traditional Slavophile ideas and discourse (since Peter the Great), neo-Eurasianists are convinced that the days of western world leadership could be numbered and that Russia will replace the west.

With regards to India, Priya Chacko brilliantly navigates between traditional and revisionist perspectives on Indian foreign policy, the former emphasizing Indian versions of idealism, the latter emphasizing why India must grow up by adopting power-oriented perspectives. Her own approach is to consider foreign policy 'a self-reflexive ethico-political project of identity construction' (Chacko, 2013: 3). She emphasizes the deep ambivalences in Indian discourse on foreign policy and analyses the meta-narratives presenting India as a civilization-state embedded in civilizational exceptionalism. Unhappy with the tendency to keep analysis at a general level, she explores how ideas about civilization inform policy-making and the conduct of foreign relations, including the role of civilization discourse in reasons for action (i.e. in strategies of justification). Ever more states are thus lining up for a status as a civilization-state and/or empire, and political discourses related to inter-civilization relations are thriving. Among the main initiatives, we find Dialogue on Civilizations, Dialogue among Civilizations and the UN-sponsored Alliance of Civilizations. Given the global material power shifts and the sustained debates about normative global orders, it is increasingly clear that IR is in an after-hegemony phase. Theoretical perspectives and debates on global order have become de-centric, are conducted in several languages and constitute different discursive structures. The traditionally close relationship between discourses of practice and discourses of theory is maintained, yet with the twist that global IR theory seems to reflect (rather than shape) practices.

The seventh passage is about enhanced socialization. Discipline is about socializing newcomers into what we believe to be the core literature, which is perpetually under (re)construction because newcomers, despite or provoked by discipline, tend either to become neoclassical or to develop their own ideas. Moreover, 'theory' is a different word for abstract knowledge about the actors, structures and processes in international, world or global politics/economics/governance (choose your favourite expression here), and, although there have always been contending perspectives, the configuration of theoretical traditions has been fairly stable over time. Should we consider it a risk or a blessing that after hegemony might destabilize the traditional configuration? The obvious risk is that a new global recurring configuration may not be viable.

Combined, the seven passages to rediscover the 'global' promise not only a truly international discipline in some golden or emancipated future but also a much needed recognition of the actually existing and global discipline. The passages promise to transcend navel-gazing west-centric critiques and offer a balanced perspective on a discipline beyond centric and decentric biases. Hence, the challenge is to turn general principles into operational roadmaps that show how the discipline can be upgraded (Valbjørn, 2017; Gelardi, 2020a, b).

Conclusion

Seen from various vantage points around the world, the idea to globalize IR seems funny at best and deeply arrogant at worst. The idea is based on the premise that western scholars own, define and protect the discipline – *their* discipline. Subsequently they project their world-views, values, concepts, theories and methodologies onto the rest of the world, showing limited or no sensitivity to eastern or southern predicaments. By contrast, scholars beyond the west suffer from disciplinary hegemony and, in any case, contribute little on their own. We westerners are now full of regret and make well-intended vows to change our self-centric images of *our* discipline. We believe that the time has now come to listen to those whom we believe have no voice and those who are silenced. It is not only a funny or arrogant but also a flawed idea underpinned by deep neglect and serious selection biases. Hence, the rescuers have become part of the problem.

As described earlier, two mega-trends characterize contemporary IR scholarship: local innocence and the globalizing honey trap. I highlighted characteristics of each trend earlier and pointed to their limitations, for instance, that each is based on narrow horizons, though each is narrow in its own way. Globalizers, for instance, display little interest in how the discipline has actually evolved beyond their own horizon, such as how it develops in Japan, Russia, China, Nigeria, Mexico or India. Moreover, what does it really mean that the discipline is 'not so international' (Wæver, 1998)? The diagnosis seems to be a snapshot characterized by limited reflection on the telos. In other words, what would a truly international discipline look like? Moreover, the diagnosis simply seems wrong – is the discipline really not so international?

Having accounted for the two trends and their limitations, I turned to outline ways forward that promise a discipline that is global in approach, coverage and recognition. When considering such paths forward, it is important to keep in mind the different parameters that go into the constitutions of the discipline: key guiding research questions, theory, an organized community and so on. It would be insufficient to focus on just one of these parameters and then make general conclusions about the discipline's global attributes. Surprisingly, the solution to the problem of local and centric research turns out to be local, ethnocentric research. Moreover, diversity remains a challenge, but especially regarding attempts to define a core of the discipline and its boundaries. If the discipline is dynamic – and this seems to be the case – then the challenge is to define a changing core and changing boundaries, the latter defined by means of key characteristics and an examination of the disciplinary contexts in which IR exists and develops.

Conclusion

What is International Relations? The previous chapters present in many ways a synthesis of an archipelago of insights about the discipline of IR, a discipline that is not always recognized or appreciated but that is practised by thousands of scholars around the world daily. I have drawn on, reproduced, reconstructed and combined a rich collection of ideas about the key parameters of disciplines in general, with an eye to the IR discipline. As highlighted on the first page of the book, it is a more than 60,000-word-long invitation to join a new understanding of IR, that is, to join a novel platform for understanding IR as a human science – as a global and diverse discipline that is 'fully-fledged, full-blown, autonomous, intellectually legitimate and accomplished' (Puchala, 2003: 273). What in this context is also worth repeating is Lynn Hunt's (1994) claim – to some a provocative claim – that disciplines have virtue. The previous pages have shown numerous examples of IR's virtue. With the seven key concepts that go into the structure of the book, the design of the platform and thus the understanding of IR as a mature discipline has seven pillars.[1]

It would not have been possible to reach the synthesis or to draw the following conclusions without guidance, which has been provided by four premises. The first premise I attribute to Martin Wight (1991), according to whom one of the main purposes of university education 'is to escape from the *Zeigeist*' (p. xx). Thereby, as Hedley Bull points out, Wight provided 'an antidote to the self-importance and self-pity that underlie the belief of each generation that its own problems are unique' (cited in Wight, 1991: xx). This book is informed by an objective similar to Wight's, that is, to escape the Zeitgeist in its many guises. It is by means of getting under the skin of key concepts that it is possible to avoid getting trapped in bland survey analysis or statistical studies that skate on thin conceptual ice. Only by genuine historical analysis is it possible to escape the increasingly popular practices of temporal provincialization, that is, imposing contemporary sets of values on the past. We should further develop our professional historical consciousness, getting to know the trajectories of the discipline not only in our own individual courtyards but worldwide. Otherwise, it will be impossible to make informed strategic decisions about future directions.[2]

The second premise is that conceptual analysis represents an underexploited resource. To make use of this valuable resource, the chapters about the nature and dynamics of the discipline have simply selected seven well-known, essentially contested concepts, deployed them in individual chapters and turned their explosive qualities into fruitful, analytical features. Each concept turned out to have qualities that transcend the symbolic and shallow deployment that often is their fate. Hence, the terms we use matter, and it is easy to underestimate the degree to which they matter. The chapters therefore include a basic explication of the key terms used in debates on discipline and diversity. Without this, we would just reproduce existing wisdom in an uncritical fashion, and that is not a worthwhile project for academics. I readily admit that there might be other important concepts we can use to explore the discipline, but that does not imply that those selected are unimportant.

The third premise is that discipline means discipline. Hence, disciplinary studies should consider the entire infrastructure of disciplines, consisting of conventions/conferences, associations, specialized journals, a body of research literature, specialized discourses, textbooks, book series and mythologies of origin as well as what Ted Hopf (2002) calls 'a particular *well-known consensually foundational literature*' (p. x). Moreover, it would be a big mistake to forget the scholarly IR community, including its (changing) norms, standards and values. However, disciplinary studies are rarely comprehensive and do not always reject the temptation to generalize on the basis of partial insights. One example is studies that focus on disciplinary communication, specifically journal publication. They are increasingly popular and occasionally produce great insights.

Yet they are obviously limited to just one part of the disciplinary infrastructure, for which reason analysts should resist the temptation to draw general conclusions about the discipline. The temptation to generalize on the basis of a partial analysis is also demonstrated, time and again, in studies on theoretical developments, including the changing configurations of theoretical orientations, as if discipline were only about theoretical reflection.

The fourth premise is that the way forward is not always to subscribe to new ideas. Occasionally, it is sufficient and even more promising to reconsider old ideas in a new context. The general reason for this being so is that historical origins are, or rather can be, the beginning of futures. Hedley Bull emphasizes this issue in his controversial argument that scholarly progress is only the second most important objective. According to Bull (1972), the first objective is to avoid forgetting existing insights. Ironically, Bull's insight turned out to be among the most forgotten insights, and replaced by the fetish of perpetually searching for something new, for advances and for the added value of what we do. There is thus a fine line between reproducing existing wisdom and searching for new knowledge.

The subject matter of the discipline is a two-faced beast in the sense that, on the one hand, it is our object of research and, on the other hand, it is frequently used to define the discipline. Given that world or global affairs evolve over time, it would be very risky to freeze the subject matter somewhere in time, thereby creating a historical bubble. Hence, war and peace may be constant and vital issues, but cybersecurity and climate change, for instance, represent novel subject matters that the discipline cannot and should not avoid. Conversely, many use subject matter to define the discipline, a procedure that brought IR into dire straits characterized by limited returns and endless debates. While it is no comfort that other disciplines were in the same straits at some point, what they did may serve as a hint of what we could do. The proposal to consider complementing or substituting subject matter with guiding research questions has been on the agenda in the past (Marchant, 1957), but at the time it was a floating idea that was not widely picked up and, seemingly, it was unrelated to research on the nature of scientific disciplines, the functions they perform and their inherently dynamic characteristics. A more sustained grounding in such research may enable fruitful debates about the relative merits of subject matter or questions asked as components of what it means to be a discipline. Likewise, the brief outline of the discipline defined by questions functions as a feasibility study that indicates that further examination would be worthwhile.

Introducing the idea of IR as a human science is also hardly a new idea. After all, it is 30 years since Ferguson and Mansbach (1988) proposed the reconsideration of the value of humanistic approaches (see also Alker, 1996). Likewise, it is almost two decades since Puchala (2003) explored the theory–history nexus in an eminent and very comprehensive fashion. More recently, Rosenberg (2016) argues that an IR outside the prison of Political Science would be a much more potent discipline, not least because it would be possible to draw on or to align it with the humanities. Thus, while it is not a new idea, it belongs to the package of ideas that would help (re)define the nature of IR – what it is all about and how it can be practised. Moreover, it is an idea that should be seen in context. We have seen how historically IR came from a number of root disciplines and, through processes of identity formation and secession, established itself as an autonomous discipline. However, particularly in the US and especially through the formative years, IR was defined as a social science, and a very narrow conception of a social science too. Its identity became something that was taken for granted: on the one hand, a symbolic pointer that ceased to produce specific criteria about what it takes to do social science and, on the other hand, undisputable conventions about what real social science is, typically focusing on quantitative methodologies. Humanistic preoccupations were abandoned until a number of 'turns' brought them back in, such as the linguistic turn, as well as cultural, normative and historical turns. Nonetheless, apart from the special case of North America, the discipline as such was more than a social science and never really severed links to disciplines within the humanities. In the present context, the growth and actually existing sociology of the discipline makes the idea of IR as a narrowly conceived social science unsustainable. Rather than suggesting an excommunication of the non-social scientists from the discipline, the book suggests that we reconsider the social and human mansion of which IR occupies one of the many rooms. As both the social sciences and the humanities currently find themselves in troubled waters, the reconciliation process will not be easy, but the increasing external pressures will presumably help generate innovative initiatives.

The general conclusion concerning discipline is that IR is here to stay. Given the current Zeitgeist, it is perhaps counterintuitive but, as hinted, I do not reject but embrace IR as a discipline. Indeed, I believe we need *more* discipline, that is, some common guidelines that will not replace but rather *complement* our pronounced anarchistic approach to professional norms, standards and methodologies. What such standards should be requires thorough debate and, at the same time, we should avoid the worst excesses or narrow-minded attempts at disciplining the discipline. Some scholars clearly do not want to recognize the discipline, and for various reasons do not want to be part of the enterprise. That is not really a problem. They are free to go wherever they want to go and do whatever they want to do. Defining the way forward for the discipline falls to those who recognize the discipline, who want to contribute to shaping it in the years to come and to increase the capabilities of IR vis-à-vis complex contemporary and practical problems. There is certainly no shortage of complex problems currently, and therefore a rationale for inter- or multidisciplinary research. However, it may be slightly too demanding to require the individual scholar to be lawyer, geologist, strategist and environmentalist scholar who has mastered it all and shift the focus to international or global dimensions without becoming the novice in all disciplinary matters.

'What is theory?' remains one of the questions defining the discipline, and the broad range of tentative answers explain why. The tentative answers come in four different categories. The first concerns the dynamic nature of theory, that the nature of theory changes over time. Hence, the development of a portfolio of IR theories during the first 100 years has not been an easy, straightforward task. It could not be, partly because the explanandum is complex, partly because conceptions of theory change across time. In other words, development phases or sequences should be expected and prove to be a helpful heuristic tool. However, periodization has its limits, not least because it suggests a uniform development of conceptions across space, which is clearly not what characterizes the global discipline.

The second component concerns the axiom that one size fits all. Despite the widespread practice of writing about IR theory as if it were a single monolith of abstract knowledge about the substance matter, the axiom turns out to be probably the least helpful one can imagine. Instead of a monolithic conception, the *problematique* calls for differentiation. One way of differentiating it is to distinguish between the different functions a theory might serve; a second way may be to differentiate between different levels of theorizing, for example, make a distinction between theoretical traditions, paradigmatic theories (the isms) and applicable theories serving the function of guiding empirical research. In this context it also matters whether a given theory is part of either the discipline's or a subdiscipline' portfolio of theories.

The third component is to finally accept the fact that Cox's (1981) theorem is valid. Theories are for someone and serve some purposes. Indeed, let us hope so. The alternative would be that theories would lose their *raison d'être*. Masamichi Rōyama's theory of the east Asian community did rationalize imperial Japan's expansionist policies (Kawata and Ninomiya, 1964). *Dependencia* theory was meant to be for someone and for some purpose. Poststructuralist theory seems to be a perfect match for contemporary anti-science and post-truth sentiments in societies around the world. Cox's theorem can thus be understood as an invitation, not to a self-appointed knight entering the scene on a critical white horse but as an invitation to have an interesting but difficult conversation about the purpose of theory X, Y and Z, as well as whom a given theory might be for.

The fourth component is the vitally important role of theory in the power politics among disciplines. IR was in this respect not always well equipped, and those who contributed to the growth of the discipline felt they had a weak hand and initiated processes of theorizing that would alter the balance of power. It did.

While it is a trivial fact that diversity has diverse meanings, it is not at all trivial to argue that diversity and discipline can be mutually beneficial. That is the conclusion in Chapter 5. It is a conclusion and an argument that is offered as a kind of dispute settlement but that most likely will not please anybody, least of all those who argue that diversity is a threat to discipline and those who argue that discipline is a threat to diversity. Nevertheless, I believe the compatibility argument is sound and an important building block for the future growth of the discipline. Without the argument, we risk the discipline being frozen in a time bubble or, alternatively, there being no discipline.

The analysis concludes that disciplines need communities to sustain their existence. The reason for this vital role is simply that disciplines are social facts, an aspect of the social reality in which we are embedded, and are therefore fully dependent on shared understandings. Following Anthony Cohen's approach to research on communities, Chapter 6 examined what community appears to mean to its members and, furthermore, if they are able to infuse its culture with vitality and thereby construct a symbolic community that provides meaning and identity. The conclusion is a confirmative yes, at least to some extent. Questions about self, other and boundaries tend to be answered differently over time. During the first examined phase, we observed a transformation from primarily being a member of other communities (e.g. the community of historians, lawyers, philosophers or sociologists) towards increasingly feeling at home within the emerging community of IR scholars. It was a highly complex and confusing process, characterized by both diffusion and contestation of professional norms and values, for instance lawyers losing their faith in the primacy of law (discovering politics and power), or historians no longer believing in the value of pure historical analysis. At the same time, professional norms such as peer review and the Chatham House Rule were under construction. The following phases of community building were no less complex, characterized as they were by contestation of the nature of science, subject matter and epistemology. In some places, members of the community began to formally organize professional associations. Hence, processes of institutionalizing the community were kicked off, and patterns of communication were consolidated, especially within national boundaries though with some examples of transnational communication. It was during this period that the associations launched many of the discipline's specialized journals. While IR needs a community for its reproduction, not all members of the community favour IR. We have seen, for instance, how some subscribe to the image of an interdisciplinary field in which they can conduct their empirical studies. They typically find it meaningful to offer rich, multicausal explanations for the actions of one or more actors or a given process. There is a final factor that leads me to the qualified conclusion. In order to explain the role of the factor, I will begin with the fact that Japan has the third largest community of IR scholars in the world (Ikela, 2008: 5). This is an interesting fact, not least in the present context of the significance of the global community and its role in cultivating the discipline. It is known that the communities in, for instance, China, Brazil, South Africa, Russia, Turkey, India and Nigeria also are also sizeable. Such facts can be useful as evidence in support of a variety of arguments, but in the present context I will just highlight the dispersed nature of the community that provides meaning and identity to its members.

Finally, concerning the question 'What is global?' I argued in favour of moving beyond both centric and decentric perspectives and actually cherish 'local'. As it might appear contradictory, an explanation is called for. There is a fundamental difference between seemingly innocent local knowledge that might even pretend to be universal and local knowledge that is conscious about its own limits. In this context, cherishing the local means that there is no reason to be afraid of your own shadow. We all make our observations from somewhere and it is better to acknowledge the point of departure than to pretend that research can be done from everywhere. The latter assumption is futile, yet it tend to inform the calls for decentric research. Moving beyond centric perspectives means leaving innocent local knowledge behind, not only Eurocentric research to the degree that such research still exists but all sorts of centric perspectives, including Sino-centric, America-centric and other centric perspectives. According to Karl Kaiser (1965), the societal environment has an impact on scholars: 'Contrary to the popular saying, scholars are by no means always writing in ivory towers. The choice of their subjects, the methods used, their implicit and explicit value orientations are frequently connected with social and political configurations of their contemporary environment' (p. 36). Kaiser not only makes the general argument, but also shows how it works in a concrete case, specifically, in research on European integration:

> Uninhibited by the Europeans' feeling of uncertainty about the 'new Europe' or the imposing presence of traditional values, the American scholars (whose European origin, incidentally, is mostly not very remote) have felt more freely able to investigate and

theorize about political and social changes in Europe that go 'beyond the nation-state'. To them, more than Europeans, Western Europe represents a huge laboratory of change that offers unique opportunities to the social scientist of searching into the nature of modern society by observing the process of change, experimenting with and testing a set of hypotheses that could help to explain it. (Kaiser, 1965: 43)

In other words, American and European scholars are situated in different environments, and this has an impact on their scholarly practices. During the 1960s for instance, the former were more open to innovatively theorizing European integration. Kaiser's insight have wide implications. Not only do they illustrate Mannheim's idea about *Standortgebundenheit* but they also suggest that the view of outsiders might have advantages that decentrists tend to dismiss by default.

In terms of wider perspectives, I wonder if it is far-fetched to imagine a Copernican turn?[3] Instead of seeing IR as merely a field of study, a meta-discipline, an interdisciplinary site or a subdiscipline of some discipline (e.g. Law, Politics), IR could be seen as a discipline and its subfields (e.g. Political Science, Law, History, Sociology). In other words, we could work on turning the tables and, instead of seeing a discipline in prison, we could develop it as the master discipline (enjoying a dozen subdisciplines and subfields) that puts single-issue and single-level disciplines to work – the synthesizing device that brings single-aspect disciplines together. After all, IR has time and again proved capable of producing a research agenda of which no other discipline is capable. Whereas the 20th century was a century in which IR was raised, the 21st century could be the century in which IR grows up.

Notes

Introduction

1 Following convention, 'International Relations' and the abbreviation 'IR' refer to the academic study of international or global affairs, whereas 'international relations' refers to the actors, structures and processes that are being studied.

2 I will keep the founders of the discipline unspecified for now. Attaching labels like 'utopians' or 'internationalists' to them would suggest that I refer to the usual suspects, which would be highly misleading. As the following chapters will demonstrate, I have a considerably wider community in mind, and the main argument is that their mission is accomplished.

3 The group of contemporary premier disciplinary historiographers include Lucian Ashworth, Duncan Bell, Nicolas Guilhot, Ian Hall, Takashi Inoguchi, Thorbjørn Knutsen, David Long, Patricia Owens, Joanne Pemberton, Brian Schmidt, Bruno Vigezzi and Peter Wilson (see also Shimizu et al, 2008; Thakur et al, 2017).

4 In 1963 the International Studies Association (ISA) had only 60 paying members, primarily from the US west coast region. With such a small number, making bold claims about trends, schools and mainstreams is obviously very risky. Yet, it is also true that the ISA at the time represented only a small part of the IR community in the US.

5 Florence Melian Stawell's *The Growth of International Thought* (1929) provides an overview ranging from 'ancient thought' (Hellenic and Hebraic) to 'Europe after Napoleon'. Stawell points out that 'The survey which follows has been, for reasons of space, confined on the whole to Europe, but the same factors are and always have been at work in all nations' (p 7).

6 I am grateful to my colleague Gorm Harste for making me aware of this important observation.

7 In 1936 it was self-evident that 'the war' referred to the First World War. In the case of Japan, it was during the years Japan began to engage seriously in international society.

8 https://conference.bisa.ac.uk [accessed 31 March 2020].

9 The aim of the book should make it clear that I do not intend to contribute to making IR an empty signifier. By contrast, contemporary history-less scholars tend to proudly state that they have not read any IR classics, thereby repeating Henry Ford's approach to history and tradition: 'History is more or less bunk.'

10 In this context, my prime interest is in essentially contested concepts that help us understand the nature of the discipline. However, the complexity of essentially contested concepts also plays an important role in the teaching of IR. Hence, it may be that textbooks tend to have a western origin and are structured around western concepts, but the reception of key concepts seems to show significant variation around the world (see Darwich et al, 2020).

11 Subject matter is about ontology, which is as fundamental as it gets in our trade. The use of method to define the discipline is to put the cart in front of the horse; it is therefore bound to fail, as demonstrated by developments in the 1950s and 1960s as well as the 2000s.

12 Such calls include international political economy (IPE) (Strange, 1970); women (Peterson, 1992); the global public domain and its inhabitants (Ruggie, 2004); and race (Vitalis, 2015).

13 Ideas about what the two tents include tend to reflect individual analysts' (including the present author's) own experience. For a different categorization, see for example Duncan Bell (2009: 3). In this context, we should keep in mind the potential difference between disciplinary and organizational (departmental) categories.

14 Immanuel Wallerstein has an interest in what the social sciences ought to become (see Wallerstein et al, 2003). His lecture prompted some very interesting responses, including two introductions to social thought of the non-western world.

15 The nature of social science is much broader than the scientist or positivist framing of it, as seen in the sociological tradition of Weber, Simmel and Schütz.

16 The topic of scientific communities is more complex than might appear. To reduce the multiple meanings of the term 'paradigm' in his famous book, Kuhn introduced the term 'disciplinary matrix' in a postscript to the second edition, only to find out that it is no easy task to define either 'scientific communities' or their beliefs and values (see Musgrave, 1971).

17 I have a pragmatic approach to labels and therefore will not make much ado about them, focusing instead on substantive issues, among which I count symbolic meanings.

Chapter 1

1 The misgivings may reflect real trends of insular practices that surely exist, but they may also reflect the trend of subdisciplinary differentiation and thus be slightly nostalgic, that is, consist of sentiments about missing the good old days when the discipline was one and the community a cosy bunch of peers (on subdisciplinary differentiation, see Chapter 3).

2 Harry Kreisler, 'Conversation with Kenneth N. Waltz', available from: http://globetrotter.berkeley.edu/people3/Waltz/waltz-con2.html [accessed 24 June 2021].

3 Between 1928 and 1939 the ISC organized annual meetings in a number of European cities.

4 Throughout most of the 1920s, Germany was excluded from international scientific cooperation. It was therefore symbolically significant that the first meeting of the ISC took place in Berlin at the Hochschule für Politik (Pemberton, 2020). See also Korenblat, 2006; Lehnert, 1989).

5 A fair number of the scholars who promoted the study of international relations during the interwar years were scholar-practitioners, some with direct experience of the Versailles conference, such as E.H. Carr, Ludwik Ehrlich, Alfred Zimmern, Ernst Jäckh and Albert Mendelsohn-Bartholdy.

6 Methodological wideners aim at expanding the methodological repertoire, an objective that is different from the topic of this chapter, which is devoted to the subject of IR.

7 With reference to the inclusion of civilization as an important category, I do not have Samuel Huntington (1993) in mind, but rather, for example, Peter Katzenstein, who has striven to make civilization an analytical category. The same has not been done with regard to empire, but it should not be impossible, especially if drained for the current, predominantly ideological, dimensions.

8 Compare, for instance, Hakim (2000) to de Vaus (2001). A video lecture on types of research design represents an understanding similar to Vaus': www.youtube.com/watch?v=1S2siBpTPis [accessed 28 June 2021].

9 https://understandingsociety.blogspot.com /2009/07/macintyre-and-taylor-on-human-sciences.html [accessed 7 September 2021].

10 The contrast between liberal internationalists in Germany and Britain is remarkable (see e.g. Rietzler 2008; Stöckmann 2016; 2017a, 2017b; Morgan 1979; Markwell 1986).

11 Ferguson also seems to overlook studies by scholars whom Patricia Owens (2018) calls 'historical women in IR'; see also Stöckmann (2018) and Ashworth 2011c. If we go beyond disciplinary boundaries, we find that peace movements and women's role in them have contributed to the prehistory of the discipline (see e.g. Rupp 1997).

Chapter 2

1 Funders of research and think-tanks also take an interest in the role of the social sciences and the humanities (see European Commission, 2009; DEA, 2012).

2 ISC scholars considered the 'international mind' to be an antidote to the nationalist mindset that had increasingly characterized European politics during the interwar years. However, Europe was not alone in turning to nationalist politics.

3 In this context, Bevir (2017) provides an excellent overview and analysis of the emergence of modernist social science.

4 Cohen (2007) advances the slightly odd idea that IPE took off as late as 1985 (Ashworth, 2011b).

5 In this way, the discipline is a bit like the early Bob Dylan, at least as Martin Scorsese portrays him in the movie *No Direction Home: Bob Dylan* (2005).

6 For notable exceptions to the rule, see Jackson (2010) and Diez (2019). The contributors to the latter forum display contending perspectives on the defining characteristics of a scientific discipline.

7 Representing major reorientations in the community of IR scholars, the three turns are genuine turns and thus different from the various pop turns that amount to just a few articles and a blogpost addressing a theme.

8 If the 1980s inter-paradigm debate is included, the positivism–postpositivism debate can be considered not the third but the fourth great debate. In any case, their contested nature and non-global characteristics suggest that the 'great debates' should probably be downgraded to just 'debates' and thus stripped of their disciplinary progress credentials.

9 For a critique of Taylor, see Kincaid (2012).

10 This does not of course exclude the possibility of taking an anti-disciplinary stance (see Rosow, 2003).

11 Martin Wight outlines his vision for the new subdiscipline, European Studies, in Daiches (1964). For a comparison between red brick and traditional universities such as Oxford and Cambridge see Smith (1985).

Chapter 3

1 In contrast to many social constructivists in IR, John Searle (1995) has a distinct take on the *objective* dimension of social and institutional facts. In other words, Searle claims that it is perfectly possible to combine claims about the objective state of affairs of social realities, on the one hand, and about social and institutional facts, on the other.

2 This is precisely how IR scholars pitch research on the genesis and development of IR.

3 John Kane makes the argument in the context of analysing the persistent tension between US foreign policy and the normative superstructure of US identity.

4 The aim of the Rockefeller Foundation-sponsored 1954 conference was to equip IR with a hegemonic theoretical paradigm: realism (Guilhot, 2011). In most parts of the world, however, the discipline took other turns, and realism achieved paradigmatic status only in the US.

5 The section draws on Jørgensen 2017b: 29–33. The present book is a 180+-page-long extension of the three pages in my textbook.

6 The emphasis on scientific studies inadvertently triggered a 'science' arms race, as the realists wanted to be more scientific and the behaviouralists believed they were ultra-scientific.

7 Other dimensions of international relations were left as casualties of disciplinary hegemony.

8 As we know from IPE, a few players often dominate a market and, as we know from sociology, both dominant players and players of less consequence have their dominant rituals, ceremonies and mythologies.

9 Department of International Relations, Central European University, available from: www.ceu.edu/unit/ir [accessed 30 June 2021].

10 With just one chapter allocated to IR, Hayward et al (2003) confirm the observation. The same applies to Gaus and Kukathas (2004), in which one chapter (out of 30) introduces IPT.

11 Many years later, Chris Brown (2014) picks up Carr's assessment of Manning: 'The simple truth is that Manning was not taken

seriously within the School community, where "big beasts" such as Popper, Oakeshott and Gellner roamed, and not simply because of his support for Apartheid in South Africa. Susan Strange and Fred Halliday, on the other hand, were taken seriously – they were among the big beasts of their day, listened to, not because of their desire to develop IR as a social science, but because they had something important and substantive to say about the world, which, frankly, Manning did not' (p. 352).

12 Among the few exceptions is Nordic cooperation in the field of IR, including the launch in 1964 of the journal *Cooperation and Conflict*.

13 This began with the closing down of the International Studies Conference in 1954 and the prioritizing of support to IPSA (Long, 2005; 2006; Pemberton, 2020). Some 60 years after, UNESCO still does not recognize IR as a scientific discipline (see UNESCO Institute for Statistics, 2015). If this non-recognition only had consequences within UNESCO, the damage would be limited. However, as Jesús Martínez-Frías and David Hochberg (2007) point out, UNESCO's classification has become an international standard, 'an essential international guide for many organisations and research institutions, which use it for a whole variety of purposes, for example for definition of research guidelines, cataloguing thematic projects, advertising research positions with public bodies, categorising scientists for subsequent scientific evaluations, and so on' (p. 315; see also UNESCO Institute for Statistics, 2015).

Chapter 4

1 Morgenthau (1948) describes what, in his view, a realist theory is. By contrast, Thompson (1955) examines the building blocks Morgenthau uses to build his theory. In both cases, the theme is the content of theory, not the functions of theory for the discipline (and beyond). The latter theme gets Morgenthau's attention in a brilliant essay, 'The Intellectual and Political Functions of a Theory of International Relations', first published in 1962 and subsequently republished several times (Morgenthau, 1962).

2 In the relationship between theory and reality, matching is not about naturalistic one-to-one representation, but rather abstractions that represent reality. Waltz, for instance, went to great lengths to emphasize this. At the same time, he kept insisting that his neorealist theory is a more accurate image of international politics than competing alternatives.

3 Most contemporary professional IR associations are still national and cater to national markets rather than to transnational or global markets. Government agencies across the world have other priorities, which are informed exclusively by idioms and paradigms drawn from the natural sciences: publishing in top-tier journals (in English) and doing so on the cheap, without having to invest in appropriate teacher-student ratios or suitable production facilities.

4 Wight's three traditions are realism, rationalism and revolutionism, presented as timeless, ideational constructs, each characterized by recurrence and repetition; alas, 'traditional' traditions. Contemporary forms are typically called realism (Hobbes), English School or the international society tradition (Grotius) and liberalism (Kant), with the intellectual godfathers in parenthesis. However, if one compares Wight's canon of rationalist thinkers and the canon of classical liberal philosophers, the overlap is striking.

5 In terms of actors that are external to higher education institutions, it is worth noting that the EU funding scheme used to allocate a mere 3 per cent to the human sciences; under the current Horizon Europe programme the EU has abandoned even the tiny quota.

6 Compare, for example, a theory-generating subdiscipline such as security studies to less capable theory-generating fields such as European studies or regionalization studies, the latter of which is still circling around definitional matters.

7 On the nature of public philosophies, see Weir (1992) and Schumaker (2008).

Chapter 5

1 Adesina draws on Thakur et al (2017).

2 Both Peter Katzenstein (2011) and Henry Nau (2011) took issue with Lake's condemnation of the 'isms', arguing that they are unavoidable and actually serve important functions. Moreover, replacing multiple isms with a new ism also seems not to be the best means to enhance understanding and progress. What is interesting is that Richard K. Ashley and Robert Walker 20 years before Lake also were critical of paradigms and employed a religious discourse writing about "a loss of faith, a degeneration of reigning paradigms" (Ashley and Walker, 1990b: 259–68).

3 'Problematic' is typically deployed to signal that contestation would be considered highly inappropriate. Conversations should be inclusive but not inclusive in the wrong sense.

4 According to Schopenhauer, eristic yelling is not merely yelling but much darker and full of symbolic violence. I owe this observation to Mateusz Filary-Szczepanik.

5 With the attempted defamation of securitization theorists Ole Wæver and Barry Buzan, 'racism' can be added to the list. In their defence, Wæver and Buzan (2020) use professional codes of conduct to discipline the defaming authors and the journal editors who are seemingly unaware of the discipline's norms or believe that they do research beyond the discipline's boundaries.

6 In the context of teaching IR in the Middle East, Salloukh and Hazbun address the issue of teaching a core literature yet emphasize that the core or mainstream literature should not be taught as an etched-in-stone doxa (see Darwich and Kaarbo, 2020).

Chapter 6

1 https://en.wikipedia.org/wiki/Institute_of_Pacific_Relations

2 Manning (1962a) adds: 'It is hard to exaggerate what that opportunity could mean to those, like Lucy Mair, and Bailey, and Lauterpacht, who understood how best to use it. There are teachers now on the staff [at the London School of Economics] who have never had a comparable experience' (p. 353). On Mair's conception of colonial administration as a science and her move to social anthropology, see Mair, 1933; 2004; Owens 2018: 476–9; Davis 2021.

3 While offering a brilliant analysis of early disciplinary work, it seems to me Andreas Osiander (1998) is too bold in concluding that a professional academic community 'did not exist in any very meaningful way' (p. 427). Whether or not a community exists obviously depends on the criteria one applies.

4 On Ehrlich, see Hachkevych (2017).

5 Some might wonder about my selection of the three transnational examples. Why not include other examples? The answer is simple. During the interwar years, there were no other major examples of transnational disciplinary community building. Transnational interaction of international organizations and non-state actors is a different issue and a rich research agenda that would include socialist and communist international cooperation (see Laqua 2011; 2015). That a *Handbook of Institutions for the Scientific Study of International Relations*, covering 12 countries, could be published before 1930 by the League of Nations Institute for Intellectual Cooperation (1929) suggests a remarkable increase in institutions and staff.

6 The assessment is based on the membership of professional associations worldwide; among the 25 members of WISC, for

instance, are South Korea (1,200 members), US (6000), UK (1,000), Europe (1,500), Mexico, Philippines, Russia, Brazil, India and Japan. As Josuke Ikeda (2008) points out, Japan has the third largest community of IR scholars in the world. China is a big unknown.

7 The ISA responded in an 'explorative' mode to the launch of EISA and in a caustic mode to the institutionalization of WISC.

8 https://academic.oup.com/isr/pages/General_Instructions [accessed 7 September 2021].

9 See for instance Friedersdorf (2018). The case reminds me of a 1990s process (see Bernstein, 1994) but clearly is part of a much wider *problematique* (see Petrina, 2012).

Chapter 7

1 One reviewer confirms the potential gap in all texts between author intent and reader reception, believing that the employment of the term *terroiriste* is some kind of (poor) in-joke, an example of humour in poor taste. The chapter is about the nexus between geographical location and theory and discipline building. The use of the term *terroiriste* is inspired by Mike Veseth's great book *Wine Wars: The Curse of the Blue Nun, the Miracle of the Two Buck Chuck, and the Revenge of the Terroirists* (2011). Readers with an interest in the topic will also enjoy watching Jonathan Nossiter's *Mondovino*, a documentary about the globalization of wine production and consumption. I should like to add that my widespread use of the term 'theorist' is also not intended as an in-joke; it is simply a term I use for scholars who engage in theory building, in practices of theorizing.

2 The idea of hegemony plays a prominent role in Rosenau's *Global Voices. Dialogues in International Relations* (1993). A book that makes an intriguing and enjoyable read, it provides a glimpse of the early 1990s *ambiente* but with its American and British contributors there is, as pointed out by Rita Abrahamsen (2007), a selection issue that makes the book title slightly misleading.

3 Other scholars also had difficulties acknowledging the existence of hegemony, an issue William Wallace addressed in a keynote speech at a BISA conference in York (Wallace, 1996; see also Smith's response: Smith, 1997).

4 An article entitled 'Continental IR Theory: the best kept secret' (Jørgensen, 2000) prompted, with some justification, the wry comment: 'What continent?'

5 Subscribers to the journal *Foreign Affairs* are requested to situate themselves, the options being American, Canadian and international.

6 In their introduction to Hans Morgenthau's *The Concept of the Political*, Hartmut Behr and Felix Rösch (2013) provide a fine explication of the concept. In short, the concept refers to how a given theoretical perspective is bounded or framed by the environment in which it originates. It is a different matter if the birthmarks of a theory or concept make it inapplicable in wider contexts or even universally. For instance, the Venetian origin of the term 'ghetto' seems not to make it universally inapplicable. Quite the contrary.

7 By contrast, IR literature has been much less efficient in this respect and tends to focus *only* on discriminatory ethnocentrism. I wonder which local conditions prompt IR scholars to such a systematically biased focus.

8 While the discovery of 'a not so international discipline' (Wæver, 1998) prompted the book series Worlding Beyond the West, Hobson's (2012) admonishment of Eurocentrism prompted the book series Global Dialogues: Non-Eurocentric Visions of the Global, coedited by John Hobson and L.H.M. Ling.

9 The irony is that it is exactly the 19th-century state of affairs – international power politics – that the EU aims at transcending both domestically (i.e. within Europe) and internationally.

10 In a sense, such preoccupations mirror the introverted EU institutions, which are obsessed or overwhelmed by enlargement, treaty reform processes or the domestic implosion of the EU's liberal values.

11 Tickner and Wæver (2009) reach their conclusions about state-centrist and realism-informed studies being widespread around the world on the basis of 17 chapters. Their book is among the first that in a comprehensive fashion shows an interest in disciplinary practices around the world.

12 The section draws on K.E. Jørgensen (2017a).

13 The 2001 Hong Kong Convention of International Studies, 26–28 July 2001. Some 700 scholars addressed the theme 'Globalization and its Challenges in the 21st Century', www-1.hku.hk/press/c_news_detail_4740.html [accessed 2 July 2021].

14 It should be noted that occidentalism comes in different versions, compare for instance Mohamed (2015) to Buruma and Margalit (2004).

15 The Palgrave Macmillan book series Trends in European IR Theory aims at reconstructing the major IR theoretical traditions

in Europe. The first of nine volumes, *Reappraising European IR Theoretical Traditions* (see Jørgensen et al, 2017), sets the agenda. Each volume in the series simply reviews what has come out of Europe but does not engage in comparisons with other parts of the world and therefore is unable to conclude anything about distinctly European traditions.

16 For six years, Dugin was head of the Department of the Sociology of International Relations at Moscow University. For a brief introduction to his ideas, see Dugin (2014b); see also Shlapentokh (2007).

Conclusion

1 I guess designing the IR mansion in this fashion is an example of genuine research design which thus stands in stark contrast to the hijacked version of research design that strictly focuses on hair-splitting exercises in technicalities. For a similar understanding of research design, see Catherine Hakim (2000).

2 Previous examples of retrospect and prospect analysis include Reynolds (1975), which was occasioned by the launch of the *British Journal of International Studies*.

3 To the best of my knowledge, Hoffmann (1959: 347) was the first to ask the question. However, his plea did not gain much traction. Six decades later, it may be the right time to reconsider responses.

References

Aalto, P., Harle, V. and Moisio, S. (eds) (2011) *International Studies: Interdisciplinary Approaches*, New York: Springer.

Abdelkader, D., Adiong, N. and Mauriello, R. (eds) (2016) *Islam and International Relations: Contributions to Theory and Practice*, New York: Springer.

Abrahamsen, R. (2007) 'Postcolonialism', in M. Griffiths (ed.) *International Relations Theory for the Twenty-First Century: An Introduction*, Abingdon: Routledge, pp 111–22.

Acharya, A. and Buzan, B. (2007) 'Preface: why is there no non-western IR theory: reflections on and from Asia', *International Relations of the Asia-Pacific*, 7(3): 285–6.

Achcar, G. (2008) 'Orientalism in reverse', *Radical Philosophy*, 152: 20–30.

Adams, J., Keane, W. and Dutton, M. (2005) *The Politics of Method in the Human Sciences: Positivism and its Epistemological Others*, Durham, NC: Duke University Press.

Adesina, O.S. (2020) 'International relations and the quest for African voice', *African Journal for the Psychological Studies of Social Issues*, 23(1): 198–223.

Adler, E. and Pouliot, V. (2011) 'International practices', *International Theory*, 3(1): 1–36.

Akami, T. (2001) *Internationalizing the Pacific: The United States, Japan, and the Institute of Pacific Relations in War and Peace, 1919–45*. London: Routledge.

Alagappa, M. (2011) 'International relations studies in Asia: distinctive trajectories', *International Relations of the Asia-Pacific*, 11(2): 193–230.

al-Azm, S.J. (1981) 'Orientalism and orientalism in reverse', *Khamsin*, 8: 5–26.

Albert, M. and Buzan, B. (2017) 'On the subject matter of international relations', *Review of International Studies*, 43(5): 898–917.

Alejandro, A. (2017a) 'International relations and foreign policy in India: policy-oriented works between discipline and state', in M. Hansel, R. Khan and M. Levaillant (eds) *Theorizing Indian Foreign Policy*, Abingdon: Routledge, pp 39–56.

Alejandro, A. (2017b) 'Eurocentrism, ethnocentrism, and misery of position: international relations in Europe: a problematic oversight', *European Review of International Studies*, 4(1): 5–20.

Alejandro, A. (2017c) 'The narrative of academic dominance: how to overcome performing the "core–periphery" divide', *International Studies Review*, 19: 300–4.

Alejandro, A. (2018) *Western Dominance in International Relations? The Internationalisation of IR in Brazil and India*, London: Routledge.

Alker, H.R. (1996) *Rediscoveries and Reformulations: Humanistic Methodologies for International Studies*, Cambridge: Cambridge University Press.

Allan, P. and Goldman, K. (eds) (1992) *International Relations Theory After the Cold War*, The Hague: Kluwer.

Amin, S. (1989) *Eurocentrism: Modernity, Religion, and Democracy: A Critique of Eurocentrism and Culturalism*, New York: NYU Press.

Amstrup, N. (1989) 'The study of international relations: old or new? A historical outline (1500 to 1939)', Working Paper, Aarhus: Department of Political Science, Aarhus University.

Anderson, B. (1991) *Imagined Communities: Reflections on the Origin and Spread of Nationalism*, London: Verso.

Anderson, M.R. (2009) 'Pacific dreams: the Institute of Pacific Relations and the struggle for the mind of Asia', doctoral dissertation, University of Texas at Austin.

Anderson, P. (1973) *Considerations on Western Marxism*, London: Verso.

Andrén, N. (1965) 'Introduction', *Cooperation and Conflict*, 1(1): 1–5.

Armitage, D. (2004) 'The fifty years' rift: intellectual history and international relations', *Modern Intellectual History*, 1(1): 97–109.

Armitage, D. (2012) *Foundations of Modern International Thought*, Cambridge: Cambridge University Press.

Aron, R. (1962/1966) *Peace and War: A Theory of International Relations*, New York: Doubleday.

Aron, R. (1967) 'What is a theory of international relations?', *Journal of International Affairs*, 21: 185–206.

Ashley, R.K. and Walker, R.B.J. (1990a) 'Reading dissidence/writing the discipline: crisis and the question of sovereignty in international studies', *International Studies Quarterly*, 34(3): 367–416.

Ashley, R.K. and Walker, R.B.J. (1990b) 'Speaking the language of exile: dissident thought in international studies', *International Studies Quarterly*, 34(3): 259–68.

Ashworth, L.M. (2011a) 'Realism and the spirit of 1919: Halford Mackinder, geopolitics and the reality of the League of Nations', *European Journal of International Relations*, 17(2): 279–301.

Ashworth, L.M. (2011b) 'Missing voices: critical IPE, disciplinary history and H.N. Brailsford's analysis of the capitalist international anarchy', in S. Shields, I. Bruff and H. Maccartney (eds) *Critical International Political Economy*, London: Palgrave Macmillan, pp 9-26.

Ashworth, L.M. (2011c) 'Feminism, war and the prospects for peace: Helena Swanwick (1864–1939) and the lost feminists of inter-war international relations', *International Feminist Journal of Politics*, 13(1): 25–43.

Austin, J.L. (1962) *How to Do Things with Words*, Oxford: Oxford University Press.

Aydinli, E. and Biltekin, G. (eds) (2018) *Widening the World of International Relations: Homegrown Theorizing*, London: Routledge.

Aydinli, E. and Mathews, J. (2000) 'Are the core and periphery irreconcilable? The curious world of publishing in contemporary international relations', *International Studies Perspectives*, 1(3): 289–303.

Ball, T. (1995) *Reappraising Political Theory: Revisionist Studies in the History of Political Thought*, Oxford: Clarendon Press.

Banks, M. (1985) 'The inter-paradigm debate', in M. Light and A.J.R. Groom (eds) *International Relations: A Handbook of Current Theory*, London: Frances Pinter, pp 7–26.

Baron, I.Z. (2015) 'IR has not, is not and will not take place', *International Relations*, 29(2): 259–63.

Barthes, R. (1957) *Mythologies*, New York: Hill & Wang.

Behr, H. and Rösch, F. (2013) 'Part I, Introduction', in H. Behr and F. Rösch (eds), Hans J. Morgenthau, *The Concept of the Political*, London: Palgrave, pp 1–79.

Bell, D.S.A. (2001) 'International relations: the dawn of a historiographical turn?' *British Journal of Politics and International Relations*, 3(1): 115–26.

Bell, D. (2009) 'Writing the world: disciplinary history and beyond', *International Affairs*, 85(1): 3–22.

Berenskoetter, F. (2012) 'The end of IR theory as we know it …', The Disorder of Things [Blog], 3 August, available from: https://thedisorderofthings.com/2012/08/03/the-end-of-ir-theory-as-we-know-it [accessed 23 June 2021].

Berghahn, V.R. (2001) *America and the Intellectual Cold Wars in Europe: Shepard Stone between Philanthropy, Academy, and Diplomacy*, Princeton: Princeton University Press.

Bernstein, R. (1994) 'Guilty if charged', *New York Review of Books*, 13 January, available from: www.nybooks.com/articles/1994/01/13/guilty-if-charged [accessed 23 June 2021].

Bevir, M. (ed.) (2017) *Modernism and the Social Sciences: Anglo-American Exchanges*, Cambridge: Cambridge University Press.

Bevir, M. and Hall, I. (2017) 'International relations', in M. Bevir (ed.) *Modernism and the Social Sciences: Anglo-American Exchanges*, Cambridge: Cambridge University Press, 130–54.

Bevir, M. and Hall, I. (2020) 'Interpreting the English school: history, science and philosophy', *Journal of International Political Theory*, 16(2): 120–32.

Bilgin, P. (2017) 'Inquiring into others' conceptions of the international and security', *PS: Political Science & Politics*, 50(3): 652–5.

Bleiker, R. (1997) 'Forget IR theory', *Alternatives*, 22(1): 57–86.

Bloch, J.G. (1898) *La guerre future*, Paris: Paul Dupont.

Bozeman, A.B. (1960) *Politics and Culture in International History*, Piscataway, NJ: Transaction.

Braudel, F. (1972) *The Mediterranean and the Mediterranean World in the Age of Philip II*, trans. S. Reynolds, Berkeley: University of California Press.

Braybrooke, D. (ed.) (1965) *Philosophical Problems of the Social Sciences*, London: Macmillan.

Brown, C. (2001) 'Fog in the Channel: continental relations theory isolated (or an essay on the paradoxes of diversity and parochialism in IR theory)', in R.M.A. Crawford and D.S.L. Jarvis (eds) *International Relations: Still an American Social Science? Towards Diversity in International Thought*, Albany: State University of New York Press, pp 203–19.

Brown, C. (2014) 'IR as a social science: a response', *Millennium*, 43(1): 351–4.

Bryce, J. (1922) *International Relations*, Port Washington, WA: Kennikat Press.

Bueger, C. and Gadinger, F. (2014) *International Practice Theory: New Perspectives*, London: Palgrave Macmillan.

Bull, H. (1969) 'International theory: the case for a classical approach', in K. Knorr and J.N. Rosenau (eds) *Contending Approaches to International Politics*, Princeton: Princeton University Press, pp 20–38.

Bull, H. (1972) 'The theory of international politics, 1919–1969', in B. Porter (ed.) *The Aberystwyth Papers*, London: Oxford University Press, pp 30–55.

Bull, H. (1977/1995) *The Anarchical Society: A Study of Order in World Politics*, New York: Columbia University Press.

Burawoy, M., Steinmetz, G., Collier, A. and Breslau, D. (2005) *The Politics of Method in the Human Sciences: Positivism and its Epistemological Others*, Durham, NC: Duke University Press.

Buruma, I. and Margalit, A. (2004) *Occidentalism: A Short History of Anti-Westernism*, London: Atlantic Books.

Butterfield, H. and Wight, M. (eds) (1966) *Diplomatic Investigations: Essays in the Theory of International Politics*, London: Allen & Unwin.

Buzan, B. (1997) 'Rethinking security after the Cold War', *Cooperation and Conflict*, 32(1): 5–28.

Buzan, B. (2019) 'Before BISA: the British Coordinating Committee for International Studies, S.H. Bailey, and the Bailey conferences', *International Politics*, 57: 573–87.

Buzan, B. and Little, R. (2001) 'Why international relations has failed as an intellectual project and what to do about it', *Millennium*, 30(1): 19–39.

Callahan, W.A. (2001) 'China and the globalisation of IR theory: discussion of building international relations theory with Chinese characteristics', *Journal of Contemporary China*, 10(26): 75–88.

Carlsnaes, W. (2015) 'The analysis of foreign policy in its historical context', in K.E. Jørgensen et al (eds) *The SAGE Handbook of European Foreign Policy*, London: SAGE, pp 30–51.

Carr, E.H. (1939/1946) *The Twenty Years' Crisis, 1919–1939: An Introduction to the Study of International Relations*, New York: Macmillan.

Carr, E.H. (1961) *What is History?* New York: Penguin.

Caso, F. and Hamilton, C. (eds) (2015) *Popular Culture and World Politics: Theories, Methods, Pedagogies*, Bristol: E-International Relations.

Chacko, P. (2013) *Indian Foreign Policy: The Politics of Postcolonial Identity from 1947 to 2004*, London: Routledge.

Cohen, A.P. (1989) *Whalsay: Symbol, Segment and Boundary in a Shetland Island Community*, Manchester: Manchester University Press.

Cohen, A.P. (1998) *Symbolic Construction of Community*, London: Routledge.

Cohen, B.J. (2007) 'The Transatlantic divide: why are American and British IPE so different?', *Review of International Political Economy*, 14: 197–219.

Cohen, R. (1997) *Negotiating across Cultures: International Communication in an Interdependent World*, Washington DC: US Institute of Peace Press.

Collier, D., Hidalgo, F.D. and Maciuceanu, A.O. (2006) 'Essentially contested concepts: debates and applications', *Journal of Political Ideologies*, 11(3): 211–46.

Copeland, D. (2003) 'A realist critique of the English School', *Review of International Studies*, 29: 427–41.

Cox, M. (2005) 'Editor's introduction', *International Relations*, 19(3): 337.

Cox, R.W. (1981) 'Social forces, states and world orders: beyond international relations theory', *Millennium: Journal of International Studies*, 10: 126–55.

Crawford, R.M.A. and Jarvis, D.S.L. (eds) (2001) *International Relations: Still an American Social Science? Towards Diversity in International Thought*, Albany: State University of New York Press.

Czempiel, E.O. (1965) 'Die Entwicklung der Lehre von den internationalen Beziehungen', *Politische Vierteljahresschrift*, 6(3): 270–90.

Czempiel, E.O. (1986) 'Der Stand der Wissenschaften von den Internationalen Beziehungen und der Friedensforschung in der Bundesrepublik Deutschland', *PVS Sonderheft*, 17: 250–63.

Daiches, D. (ed.) (1964) *The Idea of a New University: An Experiment in Sussex*, Cambridge, MA: MIT Press.

D'Aoust, A.M. (2017) 'IR as a social science/IR as an American social science', in R. Denemark (ed.) *The International Studies Compendium Project*, Oxford: Wiley Blackwell, pp 1–34.

Dallmayr, K. and Yaylaci (2014) *Civilizations and World Order: Geopolitics and Cultural Difference*, Lanham, MD: Lexington Books.

Darwich, M. and Kaarbo, J. (2020) 'IR in the Middle East: foreign policy analysis in theoretical approaches', *International Relations*, 34(2): 225–45.

Darwich, M., Valbjørn, M., Salloukh, B.F. et al (2020) 'The politics of teaching international relations in the Arab world: reading Walt in Beirut, Wendt in Doha, and Abul-Fadl in Cairo', *International Studies Perspectives*, https://doi.org/10.1093/isp/ekab005

Davis, J. (ed.) (2021) *Choice and Change: Essays in Honour of Lucy Mair*, London: Routledge.

Davutoglu, A. (1994) *Alternative Paradigms: The Impact of Islamic and Western Weltanschauungs on Political Theory*, Lanham, MD: University Press of America.

de Carvalho, B., Leira, H. and Hobson, J.M. (2011) 'The big bangs of IR: the myths that your teachers still tell you about 1648 and 1919', *Millennium: Journal of International Studies*, 39(3): 735–58.

DEA (2012) *The Social Sciences and the Humanities: Use It, Don't Lose It*, Copenhagen: DEA.

Deudney, D. (2000) 'Geopolitics as theory: historical security materialism', *European Journal of International Relations*, 6(1): 77–107.

de Vaus, D. (2001) *Research Design in Social Research*, London: SAGE.

de Wilde, J. (1991) *Saved from Oblivion: Interdependence Theory in the First Half of the 20th Century*, Aldershot: Dartmouth.

Diez, T. (2019) 'Abhängige oder Vorreiterin? Zur Rolle der Internationalen Beziehungen in den Sozialwissenschaften', *ZIB Zeitschrift für Internationale Beziehungen*, 26(2): 106–53.

Donelan, M. (ed.) (1978) *The Reason of States: A Study in International Political Theory*, London: Routledge.

Dugin, A. (2014a) *Eurasian Mission: An Introduction to Neo-Eurasianism*, Budapest: Arktos.

Dugin, A. (2014b) 'Alexander Dugin on Eurasianism, the geopolitics of land and sea, and a Russian theory of multipolarity', Theory Talk #66, available from: www.theory-talks.org/search?q=Dugin [accessed 2 July 2021].

Dunn, D.J. (2005) *The First Fifty Years of Peace Research: A Survey and Interpretation*, Abingdon, Routledge.

Dunne, T. (1998) *Inventing International Society: A History of the English School*, Basingstoke: Palgrave Macmillan.

Durrell, L. (2012) *The Alexandria Quartet: Justine, Balthazar, Mountolive, and Clea*, New York: Faber & Faber.

Editorial (1999) 'Editorial: studying British politics', *British Journal of Politics and International Relations*, 1(1): 1–11.

Eldem, E. (2010) 'Ottoman and Turkish orientalism', *Architectural Design*, 80(1): 26–31.

Elman, C. and Elman, M.F. (2001) *Bridges and Boundaries: Historians, Political Scientists, and the Study of International Relations*, Cambridge, MA: MIT Press.

Elman, C. and Elman, M.F. (2008) 'The role of history in international relations', *Millennium*, 37(2): 357–64.

Ergul, F.A. (2012) 'The Ottoman identity: Turkish, Muslim or *Rum*?', *Middle Eastern Studies*, 48(4), 629–45.

European Commission (2009) *Emerging Trends in Socio-Economic Sciences and Humanities in Europe: The METRIS Report*, Brussels: European Commission.

European Journal of International Relations (2013) 'The end of International Relations theory?', Special issue, 19(3).

Ferguson, Y.H. (2015) 'Diversity in IR theory: pluralism as an opportunity for understanding global politics', *International Studies Perspectives*, 16(1): 3–12.

Ferguson, Y.H. and Mansbach, R.W. (1988) *The Elusive Quest: Theory and International Politics*, Columbia: University of South Carolina Press.

Fierke, K.M. (2010) 'Wittgenstein and international relations theory', in C. Moore and C. Farrands (eds), *International Relations Theory and Philosophy: Interpretive Dialogues*, Abingdon: Routledge, pp 83–94.

Finnemore, M. (2001) 'Exporting the English school?', *Review of International Studies*, 27: 509–13.

Finnemore, M. and Sikkink, K. (2001) 'Taking stock: the constructivist research program in international relations and comparative politics', *Annual Review of Political Science*, 4: 391–416.

Fleck, L. (1935) *Entstehung und Entwicklung Einer Wissenschaftlichen Tatsache*, Basel: Benno Schwabe.

Ford Foundation (1976) *International Relations Studies in Six European Countries: The United Kingdom, France, the Federal Republic of Germany, Sweden, the Netherlands, Italy: Reports to the Ford Foundation*, New York: The Foundation.

Fox, W.T. (1949) 'Interwar international relations research: the American experience', *World Politics: A Quarterly Journal of International Relations*, 2(1): 67–79.

Fox, W.T.R. (ed.) (1959) *Theoretical Aspects of International Relations*, Notre Dame, IN: University of Notre Dame Press.

Fox, W.T.R. (1967) *The American Study of International Relations: Essays*, Charleston, SC: Institute of International Studies University of South Carolina.

Freeden, M. (2021) 'Discourse, concepts, ideologies: pausing for thought', *Journal of Language and Politics*, 20(1): 47–61.

Frei, C. (2001) *Hans J. Morgenthau: An Intellectual Biography*, Baton Rouge: Louisiana State University Press.

Friedersdorf, C. (2018) 'Is "ladies lingerie" a harmless joke or harassment?', *Atlantic*, 9 May, available from: www.theatlantic.com/politics/archive/2018/05/is-this-old-lingerie-joke-harmless-or-harassment/559760 [accessed 2 July 2021].

Friedrichs, J. (2004) *A House with Many Mansions: European Approaches to International Relations Theory*, London: Routledge.

Gallie, W.B. (1955) 'Essentially contested concepts', *Proceedings of the Aristotelian Society*, 56: 167–98.

Gareau, F.H. (1981) 'The discipline international relations: a multi-national perspective', *Journal of Politics*, 43(3): 779–802.

Gaus, G.F. and Kukathas, C. (eds) (2004) *Handbook of Political Theory*, London: SAGE.

Geertz, C. (1973) *The Interpretation of Cultures*, London: Fontana.

Geertz, C. (1994) 'The strange estrangement: Taylor and the natural sciences', in J. Tully (ed.) *Philosophy in an Age of Pluralism: The*

Philosophy of Charles Taylor in Question, Cambridge: Cambridge University Press, pp 83–95.

Gelardi, M. (2020a) 'Moving global IR forward: a road map', *International Studies Review*, 22(4): 830–52.

Gelardi, M. (2020b) 'Blurring borders: investigating the western/ global south identity of human security', *Alternatives*, 45(3): 143–61.

Giesen, K.-G. (1992) *L'ethique des Relations Internationals: Les Theories Anglo-Americaines Contemporaines*, Brussels: Bruylant.

Giesen, K.-G. (2006) 'France and other French-speaking countries (1945–1994)', in K.E. Jørgensen and T.B. Knudsen (eds) *International Relations in Europe: Traditions, Perspectives and Destinations*, London: Routledge, pp 19–46.

Gofas, A., Hamati-Ataya, I. and Onuf, N. (eds) (2018) *The SAGE Handbook of the History, Philosophy and Sociology of International Relations*, Los Angeles: SAGE.

Goode, W.J. (1957) 'Community within a community: the professions', *American Sociological Review*, 22(2): 194–200.

Grenier, F. (2015) 'Explaining the development of international relations: the geo-epistemic, historiographical, sociological perspectives in reflexive studies on IR', *European Review of International Studies*, 2(1): 72–89.

Griffiths, M. and O'Callaghan, T. (2001) 'The end of international relations?', in R.M.A. Crawford and D.S.L. Jarvis (eds) *International Relations: Still an American Social Science? Towards Diversity in International Thought*, Albany: State University of New York Press, pp 187–201.

Groom, A.J.R. and Mandaville, P. (2001) 'Hegemony and autonomy in international relations: the continental experience', in R.M.A. Crawford and D.S.L. Jarvis (eds) *International Relations: Still an American Social Science? Towards Diversity in International Thought*, Albany: State University of New York Press, pp 151–66.

Grosser, A. (1956) 'L'étude des relations internationales, spécialité américaine?', *Revue Française de Science Politique*, 6(3): 634–51.

Guilhot, N. (2008) 'The realist gambit: postwar American political science and the birth of IR theory', *International Political Sociology*, 2(4), 281–304.

Guilhot, N. (ed.) (2011) *The Invention of International Relations Theory: Realism, the Rockefeller Foundation, and the 1954 Conference on Theory*, New York: Columbia University Press.

Gunnell, J.G. (2018) 'Meta-analysis: a philosophical view', in A. Gofas, I. Hamati-Ataya and N. Onuf (eds) *The SAGE Handbook of the History,*

Philosophy and Sociology of International Relations, Los Angeles: SAGE, pp 556–72.

Guzzini, S. (2007) 'Theorising international relations: lessons from Europe's periphery', DIIS Working Paper No. 2007:30.

Hachkevych, A. (2017) 'Ludwik Ehrlich: Cracow period of his life (1940–1968)', *Humanities and Social Sciences*, 22: 85–92.

Hacke, C. and Puglierin, J. (2007) 'John H. Herz: balancing utopia and reality', *International Relations*, 21(3): 367–82.

Haftendorn, H. (1991) 'The security puzzle: theory-building and discipline-building in international security', *International Studies Quarterly*, 35(1): 3–17.

Hakim, C. (2000) *Research Design: Successful Designs for Social and Economic Research*, London: Psychology Press.

Hall, I. (2012) *Dilemmas of Decline: British Intellectuals and World Politics, 1945–1975*, Berkeley: University of California Press.

Hall, I. (2014) 'Martin Wight, western values, and the Whig tradition of international thought', *International History Review*, 36(5): 961–81.

Hall, I. and Bevir, M. (2014) 'Traditions of British international thought', *International History Review*, 36(5): 823–34.

Hamilton, P. (1998) 'Editor's foreword', in A.P. Cohen (ed.) *Symbolic Construction of Community*, Milton Park: Routledge, pp 7–10.

Hammad, H. (2015) 'From orientalism to Khomeinism: a century of Persian studies in Egypt', *Alif: Journal of Comparative Poetics*, 35: 32–51.

Haque, E. (2012) 'Permeability of disciplinary boundaries in the age of globalization: interdisciplinary scholarship in international relations', in *Academic Demarcations: Disciplines and Interdisciplinarity*, 8, available from: www.uio.no/forskning/tverrfak/kultrans/aktuelt/konferanser/demarcations/program/book-of-abstracts-online070912.pdf [accessed 23 June 2021].

Hardon, G.H. (ed.) (2009) *Unity of Knowledge (in Transdisciplinary Research for Sustainability)*, Oxford: UNESCO.

Haslam, J. (1999) *The Vices of Integrity: A Biography of E.H. Carr*, London: Verso.

Hayward, J., Barry, B. and Brown, A. (eds) (2003) *The British Study of Politics in the Twentieth Century*, Oxford: Oxford University Press.

Hellmann, G., Wolf, K.D. and Zürn, M. (2003) *Die neuen Internationalen Beziehungen: Forschungsstand und Perspektiven in Deutschland*, Baden-Baden: Nomos.

Hobson, J.M. (2012) *The Eurocentric Conception of World Politics: Western International Theory, 1760–2010*, Cambridge: Cambridge University Press.

Hoffmann, S.H. (1959) 'International relations: the long road to theory', *World Politics*, 11(3): 346–77.

Hoffmann, S.H. (ed.) (1960) *Contemporary Theory in International Relations*, Upper Saddle River, NJ: Prentice Hall.

Hoffmann, S. (1977) 'An American social science: international relations', *Daedalus*, 106(3): 41–60.

Holden, G. (2006) 'The relationship between Anglo-Saxon historiography and cross-community comparisons', in K.E. Jørgensen and T.B. Knudsen (eds) *International Relations in Europe: Traditions, Perspectives and Destinations*, London: Routledge, pp 225–52.

Holsti, K.J. (1971) 'Retreat from utopia: international relations theory, 1945–70', *Canadian Journal of Political Science/Revue Canadienne de Science Politique*, 4(2): 165–77.

Holsti, K.J. (1985) *The Dividing Discipline: Hegemony and Diversity in International Theory*, Milton Park: Taylor & Francis.

Holsti, K.J. (2001) 'Along the road of international theory in the next millennium: four travelogues', in R.M.A. Crawford and D.S.L. Jarvis (eds) *International Relations: Still an American Social Science? Towards Diversity in International Thought*, Albany: State University of New York Press, pp 203–19.

Holthaus, L. (2020) 'The liberal internationalist self and the construction of an undemocratic German other at the beginning of the twentieth century', in J. Steffek and L. Holthaus (eds) *Prussians, Nazis and Peaceniks*, Manchester: Manchester University Press, pp 40–63.

Hopf, T. (2002) *Social Construction of International Politics: Identities & Foreign Policies, Moscow, 1955 and 1999*, Ithaca, NY: Cornell University Press.

Horkheimer, M. (1937) 'Traditionelle und kritische Theorie', *Zeitschrift für Sozialforschung*, 6(2): 245–94.

Hunt, L. (1994) 'The virtues of disciplinarity', *Eighteenth-Century Studies*, 28(1): 1–7.

Huntington, S.P. (1993) 'The clash of civilizations?', *Foreign Affairs*, 72: 22–49.

Hutchinson, P., Read, R. and Sharrock, W. (2016) *There is No Such Thing as a Social Science: In Defence of Peter Winch*, Abingdon: Routledge.

Ikeda, J. (2008) *Japanese Vision of International Society: A Historical Exploration*, Research Series, 5, Kyoto: Ryukoku University.

Ikeda, J. (2010) 'The post-western turn in international theory and the English school', *Ritsumeikan Annual Review of International Studies*, 9(3): 29–44.

Inoguchi, T. and Bacon, P. (2001) 'The study of international relations in Japan: towards a more international discipline', *International Relations of the Asia-Pacific*, 1(1): 1–20.

Institute for Intellectual Cooperation (1929) *Handbook of Institutions for the Scientific Study of International Relations*, Paris: League of Nations Institute for Intellectual Cooperation.

Jackson, P.T. (2010) *The Conduct of Inquiry in International Relations: Philosophy of Science and its Implications for the Study of World Politics*, Abingdon: Routledge.

Jackson, R. (2000) *The Global Covenant: Human Conduct in a World of States*, Oxford: Oxford University Press.

Jarvis, D.S.L. (2000) *International Relations and the Challenge of Postmodernism: Defending the Discipline*, Columbia: University of South Carolina Press.

Jarvis, D.S.L. (2001) 'Identity politics, postmodern feminisms, and international theory: questioning the "new" diversity in international relations', in R.M.A. Crawford and D.S.L. Jarvis (eds) *International Relations: Still an American Social Science? Towards Diversity in International Thought*, Albany: State University of New York Press, pp 101–29.

Jervis, R. (1998) *System Effects: Complexity in Political and Social Life*, Princeton: Princeton University Press.

Jones, R.E. (1981) 'The English school of international relations: a case for closure', *Review of International Studies*, 7(1): 1–13.

Jordheim, H. (2012) 'Encyclopedias, knowledge trees and time: interdisciplinarity and orders of knowledge', in *Academic Demarcations: Disciplines and Interdisciplinarity*, 11, available from: www.uio.no/forskning/tverrfak/kultrans/aktuelt/konferanser/demarcations/program/book-of-abstracts-online070912.pdf [accessed 23 June 2021].

Jørgensen, K.E. (2000) 'Continental IR theory: the best kept secret', *European Journal of International Relations*, 6(1): 9–42.

Jørgensen, K.E. (2014) 'After hegemony in international relations, or, the persistent myth of American disciplinary hegemony', *European Review of International Studies*, 1(1): 57–64.

Jørgensen, K.E. (2017a) 'Inter alia: on global orders, practices, and theory', *International Studies Review*, 19(2): 283–7.

Jørgensen, K.E. (2017b) *International Relations Theory: A New Introduction*, New York: Palgrave Macmillan.

Jørgensen, K.E. (2018) 'Would 100 global workshops on theory building make a difference?', *All Azimuth*, 7(2): 65–80.

Jørgensen, K.E. and Ergul Jorgensen, F.A. (2020) 'Realist theories in search of realists: the failure in Europe to advance realist theory', *International Relations*, 35(1): 3–22.

Jørgensen, K.E. and Knudsen, T.B. (2006) *International Relations in Europe: Traditions, Perspectives and Destinations*, London: Routledge.

Jørgensen, K.E. and Valbjørn, M. (2012) 'Four dialogues and the funeral of a beautiful relationship: European studies and new regionalism', *Cooperation and Conflict*, 47(1): 3–27.

Jørgensen, K.E., Alejandro, A., Reichwein, A., Rösch, F. and Turton, H. (2017) *Reappraising European IR Theoretical Traditions*, Basingstoke: Palgrave Macmillan.

Kahler, M. (1993) 'International relations: still an American science?', in L.B. Miller and M.J. Smith (eds) *Ideas and Ideals: Essays in Honor of Stanley Hoffmann*, Boulder, CO: Westview Press, pp 395–414.

Kaiser, K. (1965) '*L'Europe des Savants* European integration and the social sciences', *Journal of Common Market Studies*, 4: 36–46.

Kaiser, K. (1969) 'Transnationale Politik', in E.O. Czempiel (ed.) *Die anachronistische Souveränität*, Opladen: Westdeutscher, pp 80–109.

Kaiser, K. (1971) 'Transnational relations as a threat to the democratic process', *International Organization*, 25(3): 706–20.

Kane, J. (2008) *Between Virtue and Power: The Persistent Moral Dilemma of US Foreign Policy*, New Haven, CT: Yale University Press.

Kaplan, M.A. (1957) 'Balance of power, bipolarity and other models of international systems', *American Political Science Review*, 51(3): 684–95.

Kapoor, I. (2018) 'Žižek, antagonism and politics now: three recent controversies', *International Journal of Žižek Studies*, 12(1).

Katzenstein, P.J. (ed.) (1996) *The Culture of National Security: Norms and Identity in World Politics*, New York: Columbia University Press.

Katzenstein, P.J. (ed.) (2009) *Civilizations in World Politics: Plural and Pluralist Perspectives*, London: Routledge.

Katzenstein, P.J. (2011) 'Civilizational states, secularisms, and religions', in C. Calhoun, M. Juergensmeyer and J. VanAntwerpen (eds) *Rethinking Secularism*, New York: Oxford University Press, pp 145–65.

Katzenstein, P.J. (ed.) (2012) *Anglo-America and its Discontents: Civilizational Identities beyond West and East*, Milton Park: Routledge.

Katzenstein, P.J., Keohane, R.O. and Krasner, S.D. (1998) 'International organization and the study of world politics', *International Organisation*, 52(4): 645–85.

Kavalski, E. (2014) *Asian Thought on China's Changing International Relations*, Basingstoke: Palgrave Macmillan.

Kawata, T. and Ninomiya, S. (1964) 'The development of the study of international relations in Japan', *The Developing Economies*, 2(2): 190–204.

Kennedy-Pipe, C. (2000) 'International history and international relations theory: a dialogue beyond the Cold War', *International Affairs*, 76(4): 741–54.

Keohane, R.O. (1989) *International Institutions and State Power: Essays in International Relations Theory*, Boulder, CO: Westview Press.

Keohane, R.O. and Hoffmann, S. (1991) *The New European Community: Decisionmaking and Institutional Change*, Milton Park: Routledge.

Keohane, R.O. and Nye, J.S. (1971) *Transnational Relations and World Politics*, Cambridge, MA: Harvard University Press.

Keohane, R.O. and Nye, J.S. (1977) *Power and Interdependence: World Politics in Transition*, Boston: Little, Brown.

Keohane, R.O. and Nye, J.S. (1987) 'Power and interdependence revisited', *International Organization*, 41(4): 725–53.

Keynes, J.M. (1937) 'The general theory of employment', *Quarterly Journal of Economics*, 51(2): 209–23.

Khalidi, R. (2003) 'The Middle East as an area in an era of globalization', in A. Mirsepassi et al (eds) *Localizing Knowledge in a Globalizing World: Recasting the Area Studies Debate*, Syracuse, NY: Syracuse University Press, pp 171–90.

Khatab, S. (2006) *The Political Thought of Sayyid Qutb: The Theory of Jahiliyyah*, London: Routledge.

Kim, M.H. (2016) 'South Korea's strategy toward a rising China, security dynamics in east Asia, and international relations theory', *Asian Survey*, 56(4): 707–30.

Kincaid, H. (2012) 'Introduction: doing philosophy of social science', in H. Kincaid (ed.) *The Oxford Handbook of Philosophy of Social Science*, Oxford: Oxford University Press, pp 3–20.

King, G., Keohane, R.O. and Verba, S. (1994) *Designing Social Inquiry: Scientific Inference in Qualitative Research*, Princeton: Princeton University Press.

Knutsen, T. (2018) 'The origins of international relations: idealists, administrators and the institutionalization of a new science', in A. Gofas, I. Hamati-Ataya and N. Onuf (eds) *The SAGE Handbook of the History, Philosophy and Sociology of International Relations*, Los Angeles: SAGE, pp 193–207.

Korenblat, S.D. (2006) 'A school for the republic? Cosmopolitans and their enemies at the Deutsche Hochschule für Politik, 1920–1933', *Central European History*, 39(3): 394–430.

Kratochwil, F. (2018) *Praxis: on Acting and Knowing*, Cambridge: Cambridge University Press.

Kratochwil, F. and Mansfield, E.D. (2005) *International Organization and Global Governance: A Reader*, London: Pearson.

Kratochwil, F. and Ruggie, J.G. (1986) 'International organization: a state of the art on the art of the state', *International Organization*, 40(4): 753–75.

Kristensen, P.M. (2015) 'Revisiting the "American social science": mapping the geography of international relations', *International Studies Perspectives*, 16(3): 246–69.

Kristensen, P.M. (2016) 'Discipline admonished: on international relations fragmentation and the disciplinary politics of stocktaking', *European Journal of International Relations*, 22(2): 243–67.

Kuhn, T.S. (1962/1970) *The Structure of Scientific Revolutions*, Chicago: University of Chicago Press.

Kuru, D. (2017) 'Who f(o)unded IR: American philanthropies and the discipline of international relations in Europe', *International Relations*, 31(1): 42–67.

Kuru, D. (2018) 'Homegrown theorizing: knowledge, scholars, theory', in E. Aydinli and G. Biltekin (eds) *Widening the World of International Relations: Homegrown Theorizing*, Abingdon: Routledge, pp 59–80.

Lake, D.A. (2011) 'Why "isms" are evil: theory, epistemology, and academic sects as impediments to understanding and progress', *International Studies Quarterly*, 55(2): 465–80.

Lapid, Y. and Kratochwil, F.V. (eds) (1996) *The Return of Culture and Identity in IR Theory*, Boulder, CO: Lynne Rienner.

Laqua, D. (2011) 'Transnational intellectual cooperation, the League of Nations, and the problem of order', *Journal of Global History*, 6(2): 223–47.

Laqua, D. (2015) 'Democratic politics and the League of Nations: the Labour and Socialist International as a protagonist of interwar internationalism', *Contemporary European History*, 24(2): 175–92.

Laski, H.J. (1932) 'The theory of an international society', in Geneva Institute of International Relations (ed.) *Problems of Peace*, London: Allen & Unwin, pp 188–209.

Lebow, R.N. (2001) 'Social science and history: ranchers versus farmers?', in C. Elman and M.F. Elman (eds) *Bridges and Boundaries: Historians, Political Scientists, and the Study of International Relations*, Cambridge, MA: MIT Press, pp 111–35.

Lehnert, D. (1989) ' "Politik als Wissenschaft": Beiträge zur Institutionalisierung einer Fachdisziplin in Forschung und Lehre der Deutschen Hochschule für Politik (1920–1933)', *Politische Vierteljahresschrift*, 30(3): 443–65.

Leira, H. and de Carvalho, B. (2018) *The Function of Myths in International Relations: Discipline and Identity*, London: SAGE.

Levy, J.S. (1998) 'The causes of war and the conditions of peace', *Annual Review of Political Science*, 1(1): 139–65.

Lijphart, A. (1974) 'The structure of the theoretical revolution in international relations', *International Studies Quarterly*, 18: 41–74.

Little, D. (2009) 'MacIntyre and Taylor on the human sciences', Understanding Society [Blog], 16 July, available from: https://understandingsociety.blogspot.com/2009/07/macintyre-and-taylor-on-human-sciences.html [accessed 28 June 2021].

Little, D. (2016) *New Directions in the Philosophy of Social Science*, Lanham, MD: Rowman & Littlefield.

Little, D. (2019) 'The sociology of scientific discipline formation', Understanding Society [Blog], available from: https://undsoc.org/2019/08/09/the-sociology-of-scientific-discipline-formation [accessed 29 June 2021].

Lizée, Pierre (2011) *A Whole New World: Reinventing International Studies for a Post-Western World*, Basingstoke: Palgrave Macmillan.

Long, D. (2005) 'CAW Manning and the discipline of international relations', *Round Table*, 94(378): 77–96.

Long, D. (2006) 'Who killed the International Studies Conference?', *Review of International Studies*, 32(4): 603–22.

Lynn, J.A. (1997) 'The embattled future of academic military history', *Journal of Military History*, 61(4): 777–89.

Lynn, J.A. (2001) 'Reflections on the history and theory of military innovation and diffusion', in C. Elman and M.F. Elman (eds) *Bridges and Boundaries: Historians, Political Scientists, and the Study of International Relations*, Cambridge, MA: MIT Press, pp 359–82.

Maher, J.H. (2019) 'Rhetoric as persistently "troublesome knowledge": implications for disciplinarity', in L. Adler-Kassner and E. Wardle (eds) *(Re)considering What We Know: Learning Thresholds in Writing, Composition Rhetoric, and Literacy*, Logan: Utah State University Press, pp 94–112.

Mair, L.P. (1933) 'Colonial administration as a science', *Journal of the Royal African Society*, 32(129): 366–71.

Mair, L. (2004) 'Interview with Lucy Mair', available from: www.repository.cam.ac.uk/handle/1810/542 [accessed 23 June 2021].

Makdisi, U. (2002) 'Ottoman orientalism', *American Historical Review*, 107(3): 768–96.

Maliniak, D., Powers, R. and Walter, B.F. (2013) 'The gender citation gap in international relations', *International Organization*, 67(4): 889–922.

Mallavarapu, S. (2010) 'Development of international relations theory in India', *International Studies*, 46(1–2): 165–83.

Manning, C.A.W. (1954) *The University Teaching of Social Sciences: International Relations*, Paris: UNESCO.

Manning, C.A.W. (1955) 'The teaching of international relations', *Political Studies*, 3: 75–6.

Manning, C.A.W. (1957a) ' "Naughty animal": a discipline chats back', *International Relations*, 1(4): 128–36.

Manning, C.A.W. (1957b) 'Varieties of worldly wisdom', *World Politics*, 9(2): 149–65.

Manning, C.A.W. (1962a) 'Out to grass – and a lingering look behind', *International Relations*, 2(6): 347–71.

Manning, C.A.W. (1962b) *The Nature of International Society*, London: London School of Economics.

March, J.G. and Olsen, J.P. (1988) *Political Institutions*, New York: Free Press.

Marchant, P.D. (1957) 'Theory and practice in the study of international relations', *International Relations*, 1(3): 95–102.

Marjanen, J. (2017) 'Transnational conceptual history, methodological nationalism and Europe', in W. Steinmetz, M. Freeden and J. Fernández-Sebastian (eds) *Conceptual History in the European Space*, New York: Berghahn Books, pp 139–74.

Markwell, D.J. (1986) 'Sir Alfred Zimmern revisited: fifty years on', *Review of International Studies*, 12(4): 279–92.

Martínez-Frías, J. and Hochberg, D. (2007) 'Classifying science and technology: two problems with the UNESCO system', *Interdisciplinary Science Reviews*, 32(4): 315–19.

McCourt, D.M. (2017) 'The inquiry and the birth of international relations, 1917–19', *Australian Journal of Politics & History*, 63(3): 394–405.

McCourt, D.M. (2020a) 'American hegemony and international theory at the Council on Foreign Relations, 1953–1954', *International History Review*, 42(3): 565–88.

McCourt, D.M. (ed.) (2020b) *American Power and International Theory at the Council on Foreign Relations, 1953–54*, Ann Arbor: University of Michigan Press.

Mearsheimer, J.J. (2001) *The Tragedy of Great Power Politics*, New York: W.W. Norton.

Mearsheimer, J.J. and Walt, S.M. (2003) 'An unnecessary war', *Foreign Policy*, 134: 50–9.

Mearsheimer, J.J. and Walt, S.M. (2013) 'Leaving theory behind: why simplistic hypothesis testing is bad for international relations', *European Journal of International Relations*, 19(3): 427–57.

Meyer, E. (1902) *Zur Theorie und Methodik der Geschichte: Geschichtsphilosophische Untersuchungen*, Halle: M. Niemeyer.

Meynaud, J. (1953) 'The teaching of political science', *International Social Science Bulletin*, 5(1): 104-12.

Mitchell, S.M., Lange, S. and Brus, H. (2013) 'Gendered citation patterns in international relations journals', *International Studies Perspectives*, 14(4): 485–92.

Mitchell, T. (2003) 'The Middle East in the past and future social science', in D.L. Szanton (ed.) *The Politics of Knowledge: Area Studies and the Disciplines*, Berkeley: University of California Press, pp 74–118.

Mohamed, E. (2015) *Arab Occidentalism: Images of America in the Middle East*, London: I.B. Tauris.

Moon, C.I. and Kim, T. (2002) 'International relations studies in South Korea', *Journal of East Asian Studies*, 2(1): 45–68.

Morgan, R. (1979) 'To advance the sciences of international politics ...': Chatham House's early research', *International Affairs*, 55(2): 240–51.

Morgenthau, H.J. (1934) *La réalité des normes, en particulier des normes du droit international: fondements d'une théorie des normes*, Paris: Librairie Félix Alcan.

Morgenthau, H.J. (1946) *Scientific Man versus Power Politics*, Chicago: University of Chicago Press.

Morgenthau, H.J. (1948) *Politics among Nations*, New York: Knopf.

Morgenthau, H.J. (1962) 'The intellectual and political functions of a theory of international relations', in Hans J. Morgenthau (ed.) *Politics in the Twentieth Century*, vol. 1: *The Decline of Democratic Politics*, Chicago: University of Chicago Press, pp 62–78.

Morgenthau, H.J. (1970), *Truth and Power: Essays of a Decade, 1960–1970*, London: Pall Mall Press.

Morgenthau, H.J. (1984) 'Fragment of an intellectual autobiography: 1904–1932', in K. Thompson and R.J. Myers (eds) *Truth and Tragedy. A Tribute to Hans J. Morgenthau*, New Brunswick, NJ, and London: Transaction Books, pp 1–17.

Morie, K. (2019) 'In search of the intellectual infrastructure of studies of International Relations: changing characteristics of the International Relations Program by the Rockefeller Foundation and its expectations', *Social Systems: Political, Legal and Economic Studies*, 22: 39–57.

Murinson, A. (2006) 'The strategic depth doctrine of Turkish foreign policy', *Middle Eastern Studies*, 42(6): 945–64.

Musgrave, A.E. (1971) 'Kuhn's second thoughts', *British Journal for the Philosophy of Science*, 22(3): 287–97.

Nagel, E. (1961) *The Structure of Science: Problems in the Logic of Scientific Explanation*, San Diego: Harcourt, Brace & World.

Nau, H.R. (2011) 'No alternative to "isms"', *International Studies Quarterly*, 55(2): 487–91.

Navari, C. (2000) *Internationalism and the State in the Twentieth Century*, London: Psychology Press.

Navari, C. (2021) *The International Society Tradition*, London: Palgrave Macmillan.

Nayak, D.M. and Selbin, E. (2013) *Decentering International Relations*, London: Zed Books.

Neumann, I.B. (2014) 'International relations as a social science', *Millennium: Journal of International Studies*, 43(1): 330–50.

Nicholson, M. (1981) 'The enigma of Martin Wight', *Review of International Studies*, 7(1): 15–22.

Nye, J. (1988) 'Neorealism and neoliberalism', *World Politics*, 40(2): 235–51.

Nye, J.S., Jr (2004) *Power in the Global Information Age: From Realism to Globalization*, London: Routledge.

Ollapally, D.M. and Rajagopalan, R. (2012) 'India: foreign policy perspectives of an ambiguous power', in H.R. Nau and D. Ollapally (eds) *Worldviews of Aspiring Powers: Domestic Foreign Policy Debates in China, India, Iran, Japan, and Russia*, Oxford: Oxford University Press, pp 73–113.

Osiander, A. (1998) 'Rereading early twentieth-century IR theory: idealism revisited', *International Studies Quarterly*, 42(3): 409–32.

Owens, P. (2018) 'Women and the history of international thought', *International Studies Quarterly*, 62(3): 467–81.

Owens, P. (2019) 'On the heirs to Agnes Headlam-Morley' [Blog], University of Sussex, available from: https://blogs.sussex.ac.uk/whit/2019/04/10/on-the-heirs-to-agnes-headlam-morley [accessed 30 June 2021].

Pan, Z. (ed.) (2012) *Conceptual Gaps in China–EU relations: Global Governance, Human Rights and Strategic Partnerships*, Basingstoke: Palgrave Macmillan.

Pellerin, H. (2012) 'Which IR do you speak? Languages as perspectives in the discipline of IR', *Perspectives: Review of Central European Affairs*, 20(1): 59–82.

Pemberton, J.-A. (2020) *The Story of International Relations*, parts 1–3: *Cold-Blooded Idealists*, Basingstoke: Palgrave Macmillan.

Peterson, V.S. (ed.) (1992) *Gendered States: Feminist (Re)Visions of International Political Theory*, Boulder, CO: Lynne Rienner.

Petrina, S. (2012) 'The new critiquette and old scholactivism: a petit critique of academic manners, managers, matters, and freedom', *Workplace: A Journal for Academic Labor*, 20: 17–63.

Puchala, D. (1997) 'Some non-western perspectives on international relations', *Journal of Peace Research*, 34(2): 129–34.

Puchala, D. (2003) *Theory and History in International Relations*, New York: Routledge.

Puglierin, J. (2008) 'Towards being a traveller between all worlds', *International Relations*, 22(4): 419–25.

Pye, L.W. (1992) *The Spirit of Chinese Politics*, Cambridge, MA: Harvard University Press.

Qin, Y. (2018) *A Relational Theory of World Politics*, Cambridge: Cambridge University Press.

Qutb, S. (2006) *Milestones*, New Delhi: Islamic Book Service.

Rawls, J. (1971) *A Theory of Justice*, Cambridge, MA: Belknap Press.

Reichwein, A. and Rösch, F. (2021) *Realism: A Distinctively 20th-Century European Tradition*, Basingstoke: Palgrave Macmillan.

Reiter, D. (2015) 'The positivist study of gender and international relations', *Journal of Conflict Resolution*, 59(7): 1301–26.

Reynolds, C. (1973) *Theory and Explanation in International Politics*, London: Martin Robertson.

Reynolds, P.A. (1975) 'International studies: retrospect and prospect', *British Journal of International Studies*, 1(1): 1–19.

Riemens, M. (2011) 'International academic cooperation on international relations in the interwar period: the International Studies Conference', *Review of International Studies*, 37(2): 911–28.

Rietzler, K. (2008) 'Philanthropy, peace research and revisionist politics: Rockefeller and Carnegie support for the study of international relations in Weimar Germany', *Bulletin of the German Historical Institute*, 5: 61–79.

Rietzler, K. (2009) 'American foundations and the "scientific study" of international relations in Europe, 1910–1940', doctoral dissertation, University College London.

Roberts, P. (2012) 'Introduction', *H-Diplo Roundtable Review*, 13(30): 2–8.

Rösch, F. (2014) *Émigré Scholars and the Genesis of International Relations: A European Discipline in America?* Basingstoke: Palgrave Macmillan.

Rosenau, J. (1993) *Global Voices: Dialogues in International Relations*, Boulder, CO: Westview Press.

Rosenau, J. and Durfee, M. (1995) *Thinking Theory Thoroughly: Coherent Approaches to an Incoherent World*, Boulder, CO: Westview.

Rosenberg, J. (2016) 'International Relations in the prison of political science', *International Relations*, 30(2): 127–53.

Rosow, S.J. (2003) 'Toward an anti-disciplinary global studies', *International Studies Perspective*, 4(1): 1–14.

Ruggie, J.G. (2003) 'Taking embedded liberalism global: the corporate connection', in D. Held and M. Koenig-Archibugi (eds) *Taming Globalization: Frontiers of Governance*, Cambridge: Polity Press, pp 243–66.

Ruggie, J.G. (2004) 'Reconstituting the global public domain: issues, actors, and practices', *European Journal of International Relations*, 10(4): 499–531.

Rupp, L.J. (1997) *Worlds of Women: The Making of an International Women's Movement*, Princeton: Princeton University Press.

Russell, F.M. (1936) *Theories of International Relations*, New York: D. Appleton-Century.

Rytövuori-Apunen, H. (2005) 'Forget "post-positivist" IR! The legacy of IR theory as the locus for a pragmatist turn', *Cooperation and Conflict*, 40(2): 147–77.

Rösch, F. (2014) *Émigré Scholars and the Genesis of International Relations: A European Discipline in America?* London: Palgrave.

Sabaratnam, M. (2011) 'IR in dialogue ... but can we change the subjects? A typology of decolonising strategies for the study of world politics', *Millennium*, 39(3): 781–803.

Said, E. (1978) *Orientalism: Western Conceptions of the Orient*, New York: Vintage.

Schmidt, B.C. (1998) *The Political Discourse of Anarchy: A Disciplinary History of International Relations*, Albany: State University of New York Press.

Schumaker, P. (2008) *From Ideologies to Public Philosophies: An Introduction to Political Theory*, Oxford: Blackwell.

Schütz, A. (1953/1962) 'Concept and theory formation in the social sciences', in *Collected Papers*, vol. 1, Dordrecht: Springer, pp 48–66.

Schwarzenberger, G. (1941) *Power Politics: An Introduction to the Study of International Relations and Post-War Planning*, London: Jonathan Cape.

Searle, J. (1969) *Speech Acts*, Cambridge: Cambridge University Press.

Searle, J.R. (1995) *The Construction of Social Reality*, New York: Simon & Schuster.

Shahi, D. and Ascione, G. (2016) 'Rethinking the absence of post-western international relations theory in India: "advaitic monism" as an alternative epistemological resource', *European Journal of International Relations*, 22(2): 313–34.

Shani, G. (2007) ' "Provincializing" critical theory: Islam, Sikhism and international relations theory', *Cambridge Review of International Affairs*, 20(3): 417–33.

Shih, C.Y. and Hwang, Y.J. (2018) 'Re-worlding the "west" in post-western IR: the reception of Sun Zi's *The Art of War* in the Anglosphere', *International Relations of the Asia-Pacific*, 18(3): 421–48.

Shih, C. and Yin, J. (2013) 'Between core national interest and a harmonious world: reconciling self-role conceptions in Chinese foreign policy', *Chinese Journal of International Politics*, 6(1): 59–84.

Shimizu, K., Ikeda, J., Kamino, T. and Sato, S. (2008) *Is there a Japanese IR?: Seeking an Academic Bridge through Japan's History of International Relations*, Kyoto: Afrasian Centre for Peace and Development Studies, Ryukoku University, available from: www.academia.edu/3133720/Is_There_a_Japanese_IR_Seeking_an_Academic_Bridge_through_Japanese_History_of_International_Relations [accessed 24 June 2021].

Shinko, R.E. (2006) 'Thinking, doing, and writing international relations theory', *International Studies Perspectives*, 7(1): 43–50.

Shlapentokh, D. (2007) 'Dugin's Eurasianism: a window on the minds of the Russian elite or an intellectual ploy?', *Studies in East European Thought*, 59(3): 215–36.

Sil, R. and Katzenstein, P.J. (2010) *Beyond Paradigms: Analytic Eclecticism in the Study of World Politics*, New York: Macmillan.

Singer, J.D. (1960) 'Discussions and reviews: theorizing about theory in international politics', *Journal of Conflict Resolution*, 4(4): 431–42.

Singer, J.D. (1961) 'The level-of-analysis-problem in international relations', *World Politics*, 14(1): 77–92.

Smith, S. (1985) *International Relations: British and American Perspectives*, Oxford: Blackwell.

Smith, S. (1992) 'The forty years' detour: the resurgence of normative theory in international relations', *Millennium: Journal of International Studies*, 21(3): 489–506.

Smith, S. (1995) 'The self-images of a discipline: a genealogy of international relations theory', in K. Booth and S. Smith (eds) *International Relations Theory Today*, University Park: Pennsylvania State University Press, pp 1–37.

Smith, S. (1996) 'Positivism and beyond', in S. Smith, K. Booth and M. Zalewski (eds) *International Theory: Positivism and Beyond*, Cambridge: Cambridge University Press, pp 1–45.

Smith, S. (1997) 'Power and truth: a reply to William Wallace', *Review of International Studies*, 23(4), 507–16.

Smith, S. (2000) 'The discipline of international relations: still an American social science?', *British Journal of Politics and International Relations*, 2(3): 374–402.

Smith, S. (2002) 'The United States and the discipline of international relations: "hegemonic country, hegemonic discipline"', *International Studies Review*, 4(2): 67–85.

Smith, S. (2008) 'Six wishes for a more relevant discipline of international relations', in C. Reus-Smit. and D. Snidal (eds) *The Oxford Handbook on International Relations*, Oxford: Oxford University Press, pp 725–32.

Song, X. (2001) 'Building international relations theory with Chinese characteristics', *Journal of Contemporary China*, 10(26): 61–74.

Stawell, F.M. (1929) *The Growth of International Thought*, London: Thornton Butterworth.

Stevens, M.L., Miller-Idriss, C. and Shami, S.K. (2018) *Seeing the World: How US Universities Make Knowledge in a Global Era*, Princeton: Princeton University Press.

Stichweh, R. (1992) 'The sociology of scientific disciplines: on the genesis and stability of the disciplinary structure of modern science', *Science in Context*, 5(1): 3–15.

Stichweh, R. (2001) 'History of scientific disciplines', in N.J. Smelser and P.B. Baltes (eds), *International Encyclopedia of the Social and Behavioral Sciences*, Amsterdam: Elsevier, pp 13727–31.

Stichweh, R. (2003) 'Differentiation of scientific disciplines: causes and consequences', in G.H. Hardon (ed) *Unity of Knowledge in Transdisciplinary Research for Sustainability*, Oxford: Eolss Publishers/ UNESCO, pp 82–89.

Strange, S. (1970) 'International economics and international relations: a case of mutual neglect?', *International Affairs*, 46: 304–15.

Strange, S. (1995) '1995 presidential address ISA as a microcosm', *International Studies Quarterly*, 39(3), 289–95.

Stöckmann, J. (2016) 'Studying the international, serving the nation: the origins of international relations (IR) scholarship in Germany, 1912–33', *International History Review*, 38(5): 1055–80.

Stöckmann, J. (2018) 'Women, wars, and world affairs: recovering feminist international relations, 1915–39', *Review of International Studies*, 44(2): 215–35.

Sylvester, C. (2013) 'Experiencing the end and afterlives of international relations/theory', *European Journal of International Relations*, 19(3): 609–26.

Tadjbakhsh, S. (2010) 'International relations theory and the Islamic worldview', in A. Acharya and B. Buzan (eds) *Non-Western International Relations Theory: Perspectives on and Beyond Asia*, London: Routledge, pp 174–96.

Taspinar, O. (2008) *Turkey's Middle East Policies: Between Neo-Ottomanism and Kemalism*, Carnegie Papers, 10, Washington DC: Carnegie Endowment for International Peace.

Taylor, C. (1971) 'Interpretation and the sciences of man', *Review of Metaphysics*, 25(1): 3–51.

Taylor, L. (2012) 'Decolonizing international relations: perspectives from Latin America', *International Studies Review*, 14(3): 386–400.

Teune, H. (1982) 'History', International Studies Association, available from: www.isanet.org/ISA/About-ISA/History [accessed 28 February 2021].

Thakur, V., Davis, A.E. and Vale, P. (2017) 'Imperial mission, "scientific" method: an alternative account of the origins of IR', *Millennium: Journal of International Studies*, 46(1): 3–23.

Thayer, B.A. (2009) *Darwin and International Relations: On the Evolutionary Origins of War and Ethnic Conflict*, Lexington: University Press of Kentucky.

Thayer, B.A. and Hudson, V.M. (2010) 'Sex and the Shaheed: insights from the life sciences on Islamic suicide terrorism', *International Security*, 34(4): 37–62.

Thompson, K.W. (1952) 'The study of international politics: a survey of trends and developments', *Review of Politics*, 14(4): 433–67.

Thompson, K.W. (1955) 'Toward a theory of international politics', *American Political Science Review*, 49(3): 733–46.

Tickner, A.B. (2013) 'Core, periphery and (neo)imperialist international relations', *European Journal of International Relations*, 19(3): 627–46.

Tickner, A.B. and Wæver, O. (2009) 'Worlding where the west once was', in A.B. Tickner and O. Wæver (eds) *International Relations Scholarship around the World*, Abingdon: Routledge, pp 342–55.

Tickner, J.A. (1998) 'Continuing the conversation', *International Studies Quarterly*, 42(1): 205–10.

Tickner, J.A. (1999) 'Why women can't run the world: international politics according to Francis Fukuyama', *International Studies Review*, 1(3): 3–11.

Tsygankov, A.P. (2008) 'Self and other in international relations theory: learning from Russian civilizational debates', *International Studies Review*, 10(4): 762–75.

Turton, H.L. (2015) *International Relations and American Dominance: A Diverse Discipline*, Abingdon: Routledge.

Tyulin, I.G. (1997) 'Between the past and the future: international studies in Russia', *Zeitschrift für Internationale Beziehungen*, 4(1): 181–94.

UNESCO Institute for Statistics (2015) *International Standard Classification of Education: Fields of Education and Training 2013*

(ISCED-F 2013): Detailed Field Descriptions, Montreal: UNESCO Institute for Statistics, available from: http://uis.unesco.org/sites/default/files/documents/international-standard-classification-of-education-fields-of-education-and-training-2013-detailed-field-descriptions-2015-en.pdf [accessed 24 June 2021].

Valbjørn, M. (2004) 'Toward a "Mesopotamian turn": disciplinarity and the study of the international relations of the Middle East', *Journal of Mediterranean Studies*, 14(1–2): 47–75.

Valbjørn, M. (2006) 'Blank, blind or blinded? Cultural investigations in international relations', in K.E. Jørgensen and T.B. Knudsen (eds) *International Relations in Europe: Traditions, Perspectives and Destinations*, London: Routledge, pp 199–224.

Valbjørn, M. (2008) *A 'Baedeker' to IR's Cultural Journey Before, During and After the Cultural Turn: Explorations Into the (Ir)relevance of Cultural Diversity, the IR/Area Nexus and Politics in an (Un)exceptional Middle East*, Aarhus: Politica.

Valbjørn, M. (2017) 'Strategies for reviving the international relations/Middle East nexus after the Arab uprisings', *PS: Political Science & Politics*, 50(3): 647–51.

van Evera, S. (1997) *Guide to Methods for Students of Political Science*, Ithaca, NY: Cornell University Press.

Vasilaki, R. (2012) 'Provincialising IR? Deadlocks and prospects in post-western IR theory', *Millennium: Journal of International Studies*, 41(1): 3–22.

Vasquez, J.A. (1998) *The Power of Power Politics: From Classical Realism to Neotraditionalism*, Cambridge: Cambridge University Press.

Vergerio, C. (2019) 'Context, reception, and the study of great thinkers in international relations', *International Theory*, 11(1): 110–37.

Veseth, M. (2011) *Wine Wars: The Curse of the Blue Nun, the Miracle of the Two Buck Chuck, and the Revenge of the Terroirists*, Lanham, MD: Rowman & Littlefield.

Vitalis, R. (2005) 'Birth of a discipline', in D. Long and B.C. Schmidt (eds) *Imperialism and Internationalism in the Discipline of International Relations*, Albany: State University of New York Press, pp 159–81.

Vitalis, R. (2015) *White World Order, Black Power Politics: The Birth of American International Relations*, Ithaca, NY: Cornell University Press.

Wæver, O. (1998) 'The sociology of a not so international discipline: American and European developments in international relations', *International Organization*, 52(4): 687–727.

Wæver, O. and Buzan, B. (2020) 'Racism and responsibility: the critical limits of deepfake methodology in security studies: a reply to Howell and Richter-Montpetit', *Security Dialogue*, 51(4): 386–94.

Wallace, W. (1996) 'Truth and power, monks and technocrats: theory and practice in international relations', *Review of International Studies*, 22(3): 301–21.

Wallerstein, I.M. (2000) *The Essential Wallerstein*, New York: New Press.

Wallerstein, I., Alatas, S., Brumann, C., Calhoun, C., Hall, J. and Madan, T.N. (2003) 'Anthropology, sociology, and other dubious disciplines', *Current Anthropology*, 44(4): 453–65.

Walt, S.M. (1987) *The Origins of Alliances*, Ithaca, NY: Cornell University Press.

Waltz, K.N. (1959) *Man, the State and War: A Theoretical Analysis*, New York: Columbia University Press.

Waltz, K.N. (1979) *Theory of International Politics*, Reading, MA: Addison-Wesley.

Waltz, K.N. (1990) 'Realist thought and neorealist theory', *Journal of International Affairs*, 44(1): 21–37.

Wang, Y. (2007) 'Between science and art: questionable international relations theories', *Japanese Journal of Political Science*, 8(2): 191–208.

Weber, M. (1904/1949) ' "Objectivity" in social science and social policy', in E.A. Shils and H.A. Finch (eds) *The Methodology of the Social Sciences*, New York: Free Press, pp 49–112.

Weir, M. (1992) 'Ideas and the politics of bounded innovation', in S. Steinmo, K. Thelen and F. Longstreth (eds) *Structuring Politics: Historical Institutionalism in Comparative Analysis*, Cambridge: Cambridge University Press, pp 188–216.

Weiss, T.G. and Wilkinson, R. (eds) (2013) *International Organization and Global Governance*, London: Routledge.

Wemheuer-Vogelaar, W., Bell, N.J., Navarrete Morales, M. and Tierney, M.J. (2016) 'The IR of the beholder: examining global IR using the 2014 TRIP survey', *International Studies Review*, 18(1): 16–32.

Wendt, A. (1992) 'Anarchy is what states make of it: the social construction of power politics', *International Organization*, 46(2): 391–425.

Wendt, A. (1999) *Social Theory of International Politics*, Cambridge: Cambridge University Press.

Wight, M. (1946) *Power Politics*, London: Royal Institute of International Affairs.

Wight, M. (1960) 'Why is there no international theory?', *International Relations*, 2: 35–48.

Wight, M. (1964) 'European studies', in D. Daiches (ed.) *The Idea of a New University: An Experiment in Sussex*, London: Andre Deutsch, pp 100–19.

Wight, M. (1991) *International Theory: The Three Traditions*, ed. G. Wight and B. Porter, Leicester: Leicester University Press.

Winch, P. (1958/1990) *The Idea of a Social Science and its Relation to Philosophy*, London: Psychology Press.

Woldegiorgis, E.T. and Doevenspeck, M. (2013) 'The changing role of higher education in Africa: a historical reflection', *Higher Education Studies*, 3(6): 35–45.

Wolfers, A. (1947) 'International relations as a field of study', *Columbia Journal of International Affairs*, 1(1): 24–6.

Wolfers, A. and Martin, L.W. (eds) (1956) *The Anglo-American Tradition in Foreign Affairs: Readings from Thomas More to Woodrow Wilson*, New Haven, CT: Yale University Press.

Yamamoto, K. (2011) 'International relations studies and theories in Japan: a trajectory shaped by war, pacifism, and globalization', *International Relations of the Asia-Pacific*, 11(2): 259–78.

Zeleza P.T. (2006) 'Beyond Afropessimism: historical accounting of African universities', available from: www.pambazuka.org/governance/beyond-afropessimism-historical-accounting-african-universities [accessed 24 June 2021].

Zimmern, A. (1934) 'International law and social consciousness', *Transactions of the Grotius Society*, 20: 25–44.

Zimmern, A. (ed.) (1939) *L'ensignement universitaire des relations internationales*, Paris: Institut International de Cooperation Intellectuelle.

Zimmern, A.E. (1953) *The American Road to World Peace*, New York: E.P. Dutton.

Žižek, S. (1998) 'A leftist plea for "Eurocentrism"', *Critical Inquiry*, 24(4): 988–1009.

Index

Hall, Ian 86–7
Hamilton, Peter 9, 107
Haque, Ehsanul 61–2
hegemony 19, 83, 90, 98, 105, 118,
  121–2, 130, 135–7
  after hegemony 19, 90, 105, 118,
    122, 130, 136
  Anglo-American 83, 90, 98,
    121–2
  as a problem 118
  western 98, 135
historicism 59–60, 103
history 2–3, 7–8, 18, 30, 32, 34,
  39–43, 48–51, 61–4, 76, 92–3, 96,
  123–4, 142, 147, 149
  diplomatic 36–7
  history of the discipline 2, 7, 46,
    48, 50–1, 67, 92, 104
  and the IR discipline 40–1, 43,
    63–4, 71
  of IR theorizing 36
Hoffmann, Stanley 8, 16, 32,
  40, 87, 95
Holsti, Kalevi 3, 13–14, 16, 70, 76,
  80, 93–4, 99, 127
  discipline in disarray 14, 94, 99
  general theory of international
    politics (TIP) movement 80
  identity of discipline 3, 93–4
  IR as a discipline 16, 93
  subject matter 13, 16
honey traps 137
Horkheimer, Max 73, 76
Hôtel Majestic 49, 68
human sciences 6, 8, 22, 30–1, 33,
  39–40, 43–5, 59, 62, 70, 76,
  79, 85–6
  and IR 30–1, 39–40, 44
Humanities 3–5, 8, 16, 18, 30,
  31–3, 36–40, 43, 45, 57,
  90–1, 142
  and the English School 33, 37, 40
  and IR 8, 18, 30–1, 36–9, 43,
    90, 142
Hunt, Lynn 8, 139

I

idealists 39, 76
identity 2–4, 7, 26, 106–7,
  116–17, 132, 134–5, 145–6
  disciplinary 20, 50
  formation of 4, 20, 31, 91, 103,
    135, 142

of IR 3, 9, 18, 32, 39, 55, 79, 91,
  116, 142, 146
politics 96, 135
India 9, 132, 135
Institute of Pacific Relations
  (IPR) 107–8, 109–10
inter-disciplinary 1, 8, 18, 55, 60–2,
  65–6, 93, 97, 117–18, 145, 147
  field of study 60, 65–6, 97
  research 8, 60–1, 97
international 2–3, 10, 23–5, 27, 29,
  43, 51–5, 61, 63, 66, 78, 84, 89,
  95, 105, 121, 123, 126–33, 136,
  137, 143
  community 106, 117
  law 23, 109, 128
  mind 32, 53, 107, 109, 118
  organization 14, 17, 25–6, 36, 58,
    68, 108, 113, 128
internationalism 55, 100, 109
international political economy 16,
  17, 25, 80, 95–6, 104, 113
International Political Science
  Association (IPSA) 53, 64, 66, 78,
  110, 130
international political theory 37, 58,
  80, 95–6, 104, 112
international politics 14–15, 24–5,
  27, 54, 64, 66, 70, 77, 79, 80,
  86–7, 109, 113, 128
  and Economics 25, 113
  scholars 109
  theory of 70, 77, 79–80, 87
international society 14, 19, 23, 25,
  34, 38, 75, 78, 87, 95
international studies 4, 54–5, 60, 96,
  110, 114, 133
International Studies Association
  (ISA) 114, 115
International Studies Conference
  (ISC) 13, 66, 68, 78, 108–10
international system 24, 55, 87,
  128
international thought 25, 30, 97, 117
interwar 50, 53, 73, 76, 86, 93, 95,
  107, 110, 114
IR theory 24, 70, 77–8, 134,
  136, 144
isms 28, 82, 93, 119, 144

J

Jackson, R. 33, 101
Japan 52, 78, 90, 111

www.ingramcontent.com/pod-product-compliance
Lightning Source LLC
Chambersburg PA
CBHW070929030426
42336CB00014BA/2593